Full of Grace

Full of Grace

An Oral Biography of
John Cardinal O'Connor

TERRY GOLWAY

POCKET BOOKS

New York   London   Toronto   Sydney   Singapore

POCKET BOOKS, a division of Simon & Schuster, Inc.
1230 Avenue of the Americas, New York, NY 10020

ISBN 13: 978-1-4165-7364-7   ISBN 10: 1-4165-7364-X

First Pocket Books hardcover printing November 2001

10   9   8   7   6   5   4   3   2   1

POCKET and colophon are registered trademarks
of Simon & Schuster, Inc.

Produced by **ELIZABETH PUBLISHING**: *General
Editor:* John W. Wright; *Executive Editor:* Alan
Joyce; *Copyediting and proofreading:* Jerold Kappes

Book design by Virginia Norey

For information regarding special discounts for bulk purchases,
please contact Simon & Schuster Special Sales at 1-800-456-6798 or
business@simonandschuster.com

Printed in the U.S.A.

CONTENTS

Pilgrimage

A Priest's Life *1*

Family

Ministry

Life

Reconciliation

Inspiration

Compassion

Justice

Nearer His God

THE STORYTELLERS

Martin Begun   Past president of the Jewish Community Relations Council.

Monsignor Thomas Bergin   Vicar for education for the New York Archdiocese.

Eileen Christian   Cardinal O'Connor's niece.

Ellen Cohen   Therapist in California.

Sister Anne Connelly   Co-vicar for religious for the New York Archdiocese.

Jon Corzine   Democratic U.S. Senator from New Jersey.

Mario Cuomo   Governor of New York from 1982 to 1994

Sister Joan Curtin   Head of religious education for the New York Archdiocese.

Brother Tyrone Davis   Head of the archdiocese's Office of Black Ministry.

John Dearie   Lawyer and a former member of the New York State Assembly.

Mary Dennehy   Mother of a Down syndrome child, Eileen.

Mother Agnes Donovan   Mother superior of the Sisters of Life.

Thomas Durkin Jr.   Lawyer in West Caldwell, N.J.

Rabbi Joseph Erenkranz   Director of the Center for Christian-Jewish Understanding at Sacred Heart University, Fairfield, Ct.

Rachel Fader   Student at Holmes Junior High School in Davis, Calif.

Monsignor Peter Finn   Rector of St. Joseph's Seminary in Dunwoodie, N.Y.

Archbishop Harry Flynn   (St. Paul, Minn.) Parish priest in New York in the 1980s.

William Flynn   Chairman of Mutual of America.

Ari Goldman   Religion writer for *The New York Times* from 1983 to 1993.

Father Andrew Greeley   Sociologist and a best-selling novelist.

Dolores Grier   Former vice chancellor of the New York Archdiocese.

Nat Hentoff   Cardinal O'Connor's biographer and an authority on civil liberties.

The Rev. John Higgins   Priest at Holy Rosary parish in the Bronx.

Monsignor Charles Kavanagh   Head of the archdiocese's development office.

Mary Ellen Keating   Former executive director of communications for the Diocese of Scranton.

Peter King   Republican Congressman from Long Island.

Rabbi Leon Klenicki   Served as head of the Department of Interfaith Affairs of the Anti-Defamation League.

Ed Koch   Mayor of New York from 1978 to 1989.

John Loud   Vice president of the Patrolmen's Benevolent Association in New York.

Jennifer Lynch   Worked in the development office of the New York Archdiocese.

Wellington Mara   Co-owner of the New York Giants football team.

"Margarita"   Pseudonym for a pregnant woman who was contemplating suicide when she met Cardinal O'Connor.

Kevin McCabe   Served as chief of staff to New York City Council Speaker Peter Vallone.

Steven McDonald   New York City police officer who was paralyzed after being shot in 1986.

Patti Ann McDonald   Steven's wife; *Conor McDonald* is their son.

James McHugh   Lawyer in Pennsylvania.

Patrick McKernan   Secretary–general of the Department of Foreign Affairs in the Republic of Ireland.

Sandi Merle   Pro-life activist in New York.

Rabbi Michael Miller   Past president of the Jewish Community Relations Council.

Joanne Mohrmann   Cardinal O'Connor's niece.

Thomas Monaghan   Co-founder of the Domino's Pizza Chain and head of the Ave Maria Foundation in Ann Arbor, Mich.

Mario Paraydes   Head of the Northeast Hispanic Catholic Center.

Dennis Rivera   President of Local 1199 of the hospital workers union in New York.

Howard Rubenstein   Head of Rubenstein and Associates, a public relations firm in New York.

Jeff Stone   Spokesman for Dignity, an organization of gay Catholics.

John Sweeney   President of the AFL–CIO.

Sal Tassone   Worked in the mailroom at the New York Archdiocese's headquarters.

Raymond C. Teatum   First deputy to the City Clerk of New York.

Hugh Ward   Cardinal O'Connor's nephew.

Mary Ward   Cardinal O'Connor's sister.

Admiral James Watkins   Chief of Naval Operations under President Reagan and chairman of Mr. Reagan's AIDS Commission.

Eileen White   Cardinal O'Connor's special counsel.

The Rev. J.C. Williams   Baptist minister and a retired Navy chaplain.

Michael Zappalorti   Brother of James Zappalorti, a murder victim.

Joseph Zwilling   Director of communications for the Archdiocese of New York.

Full of

Grace

Pilgrimage

A PRIEST'S LIFE

He was born in a row house in Philadelphia on January 15, 1920, the fourth of five children born to Dorothy and Thomas O'Connor. She was a caring, indefatigable woman who suffered from insomnia; he was a union man, a skilled painter who specialized in church ceilings. Both were devout Catholics with a strong sense of faith and justice who never spoke of the future without adding the phrase, "God willing." Together, they taught their children about prayer, faith, compassion, and love. John Joseph O'Connor inherited his parents' values (and his mother's insomnia), and never forgot his modest beginnings. To the end, he was the son of a working-class family that believed in God, prayed the Rosary, and found solace and comfort not in theology, but in faith.

Five days after his time on earth ended on May 3, 2000, the world paid tribute to him with a magnificent ceremony in one of the nation's great houses of worship, St. Patrick's Cathedral in New York. While it was a public display like few others in the history of the American Catholic Church, the preceding day had witnessed an even more extraordinary sight, that of New York's rabbis and leaders of the city's Jewish community gathered in St. Patrick's for their own salute to a man they loved as a healer and conciliator.

The liturgy for John O'Connor's Mass of Christian Burial on May 8, 2000, was no different from that of any other Catholic, no different from the funeral Masses over which he himself had presided whenever a priest in his archdiocese died. The outpouring of emotion and the prominence of the congregants, however, was extraordinary, a sign that John Cardinal O'Connor's ministry had won the love and respect of Catholic and non-Catholic alike. In the front pews of St. Patrick's Cathedral were the incumbent U.S. President, his wife, his predecessor and the two candidates to succeed him, along with other celebrated dignitaries from the world of temporal power and might. Less conspicuous were those who bore personal witness to John O'Connor's years as a shepherd—those who knew him from his years as a Navy chaplain; priests and nuns; a child with one leg, waving as the coffin passed him while balanced on a pair of crutches; parents whose children he baptized; troubled men and women he counseled; immigrants who were made welcome in a cathedral built by another generation of immigrants; union organizers who saw in him the American Catholic Church's commitment to social justice; business leaders who worked with him in educating and mentoring poor children.

Colleagues from the College of Cardinals eulogized him; family members who traced their roots to that row house in

Philadelphia, and, beyond that, to a life of poverty in Ireland, said their goodbyes to a beloved brother and uncle. And as the coffin containing the earthly remains of John Cardinal O'Connor, eighth Archbishop of New York, was carried to a crypt underneath the Cathedral's main altar, the congregants burst into applause. It was sustained and heartfelt; many wept or made a sign of the cross as the coffin passed their pew. The applause lingered after the procession disappeared from view.

So ended one of the 20th century's most memorable pilgrimages.

Though John J. O'Connor had been Cardinal-Archbishop of New York for 16 years, though he had been a national and indeed global figure, a man sought out by politicians and penitents alike, at his death he remained an enigma. Universally described as outspoken, he was, in fact, soft-spoken. Labeled, even in his obituaries, as a conservative, he refused to cross union picket lines, opposed the death penalty, and argued against government policies that hurt the poor. A Navy chaplain for 27 years, retiring with the rank of Rear Admiral and Chief of Chaplains in 1979, he was a severe critic of excessive military spending. A staunch upholder of his Church's teachings on sexuality, he personally ministered to AIDS patients in a hospital he dedicated to the care of those suffering from the disease. Often portrayed in the media as rigid and judgmental, in reality his sincerity, kindness, and unstinting generosity touched the lives of countless individuals. And it is their stories, the stories of men and women from all walks of life, Christian and Jew, friend and foe, mighty and obscure, that offer a glimpse of the John Cardinal O'Connor the world rarely saw.

Pilgrimage 3

They met John O'Connor in parishes in and around his hometown of Philadelphia, in foxholes in Vietnam, at the Naval Academy in Annapolis, Md., in St. Peter's Cathedral in Scranton, Pa., and finally in St. Patrick's Cathedral. He was their spiritual leader, their boss, their comforter, their confessor, their inspiration. His life touched theirs, and they were never quite the same. Some would insist that he was a living saint; others would credit him with saving their lives, talking them out of suicide or inspiring them to fulfill the potential God had given them. In their untold stories is the truth of John O'Connor's life and ministry.

He was a parish priest, a chaplain, a scholar (with a master's degree in clinical psychology from Catholic University and a doctorate in political science from Georgetown), a bishop and finally a Cardinal-Archbishop and Prince of the Church. The role he lived for, however, was that of priest and pastor. Even as a Cardinal, he celebrated daily Mass in St. Patrick's, heard confessions, counseled couples preparing for marriage, visited the sick, and buried the dead. Uncomfortable with the trappings of wealth and the splendor of office, he never forgot the simplicity of his childhood. His friends remember a man who was more at home with the person in the pew than with men and women of privilege whose paths he crossed in Washington, D.C., and in New York.

For most of his priesthood, which began with his ordination in 1945, he was known only to his family and colleagues and those who found him a source of inspiration, wisdom, and compassion. During the time he spent as Archbishop of New York, he was known throughout the world. His last ministry brought him to every continent, and wherever he went, he was greeted, in the words of one of his secretaries, Monsignor Gerald Walsh, as "the leader of the Catholic Church in America." He did not hold such a title. There is no such title, at least not formally. And, as a matter of fact, the New York Archdiocese is not the nation's largest, since it does not cover all of New York City—the boroughs of Brooklyn and Queens form a separate diocese. To the public, however, the title of "leader of the Catholic Church in America" was his, not because he wanted it but because it seemed to suit him.

After presidential candidate George W. Bush was criticized for speaking at the anti-Catholic Bob Jones University during the South Carolina primary campaign in 2000, he sent a letter of explanation not to the head of the U.S. Bishops Conference, not to the Cardinal-Archbishop of the nation's largest archdiocese (Los Angeles), but to John Cardinal O'Connor, the public face, the public voice, and the public conscience of the American Catholic Church. He was a natural leader and a patient teacher, a vibrant personality and a man of quiet eloquence. He was an enthusiastic preacher, a passionate voice for those the world refuses to hear, a tireless advocate for those the powerful have forgotten.

The spiritual journey of John J. O'Connor might be described as unlikely, except that, as people of faith, his flock, his friends, and his colleagues believed it was not unlikely at all. They believed that God chose John O'Connor for this memorable ministry and guided him along the way, and once you accept and believe that, John J. O'Connor's journey from row house in Philadelphia to Cardinal's residence in Manhattan is hardly unlikely. It is, in fact, the only possible journey John O'Connor could have undertaken.

As a child during the 1920s, young John was not unlike other children in the neighborhood. He talked about growing up to be a police officer, and he loved baseball. As he grew into adolescence, he enjoyed parties as much as any other teenager in Depression-era Philadelphia. The most profound influence on his life, however, was the example of his parents, whose religious faith pervaded all of their actions. His mother went blind for about a year while he was a child. She credited her devotion to St. Rita of Cascia with the restoration of her sight, and for the rest of her life, she offered a nightly prayer to St. Rita, along with a Rosary and prayers to St. Therese of Lisieux. His father, whom the Cardinal described as an "out-loud pray-er," wore his prayer book to a frazzle.

By his mid-teens, not long after transfering to West Catholic High School in Philadelphia from a public high school, John was thinking about the priesthood. He soon entered St. Charles Borromeo Seminary, a place seemingly designed to discourage all but the most faithful and strongest of spirit. John O'Connor fit that description, and he was ordained at age 25.

He never intended to be anything grander than a parish priest, and he hoped to spend his priesthood working with retarded children. He spent the next seven years teaching, serving as a high school guidance counselor, hosting a radio program, and establishing the first of many ministries for children with special needs.

He joined the Navy in 1952, a career move that was not his idea; it was his bishop's. The Korean War was under way, and Francis Cardinal Spellman of New York—the head of the Catholic Church's military vicariate—put out a call for young chaplains. John Cardinal O'Hara of Philadelphia thought young Father O'Connor ought to heed Cardinal Spellman's plea, and so he did. Little did Cardinal O'Hara know that young Father O'Connor would one day hold both of Cardinal Spellman's titles, as Cardinal-Archbishop of New York and as head of the Church's military vicariate.

Father O'Connor spent nearly 30 years in uniform, sometimes at sea, sometimes on bases on either coast. He was sent to Vietnam with the 3rd Marine Division in 1964 and served on the front lines. Like many others, he would not talk very much about Vietnam once he returned, so few details of his tour of duty there are known.

He made history in 1972 when he became the first Catholic named as a senior chaplain at the Naval Academy in Annapolis. Three years later, he was promoted to Chief of Chaplains and given the rank of Rear Admiral. He held those posts until he retired in 1979, thinking that, finally, he would return to the parish work he left behind in 1952. But even before Admiral O'Connor's retirement became official, Pope John Paul II named him a bishop in charge of the American Catholic Church's military vicariate, which ministers to Catholics in the armed services throughout the world. He went to Rome for his consecration, returned home, put in his papers, put away his uniform, and, at age 59, began a new career as one of the American Church's teachers and leaders.

It wasn't long before his brother bishops discovered that this man about whom they knew precious little held many well-informed positions and was not shy about sharing them. He played a critical role in drafting a pastoral letter on nuclear warfare and defense, arguing against positions he thought were too radically pacifist. But he also became a strong voice for economic justice and for life. The bishops of America weren't the only people who took notice of John O'Connor. In 1983, the Pope named him to head the diocese of Scranton in his native state of Pennsylvania. Finally, he was going home.

Scranton, near the coal mines that gave impetus to the Catholic-dominated Knights of Labor trade union in the 1880s, quickly adopted John O'Connor as a hometown favorite. He pledged to pay the diocese's struggling teachers a living wage, and he promised to meet with every one of the diocese's priests.

He never got the chance. When he quite literally was still settling into his new job in his home state, he received a telephone call from Archbishop Pio Laghi, the Pope's representative in America. After a few minutes of small talk, Archbishop Laghi broke the news: "By the way," he said, "the Holy Father has appointed you Archbishop of New York."

John O'Connor would later tell people that he went to Scranton thinking he would die there. He went to New York knowing he would die there. Between his installation on March 19, 1984, and his death on May 3, 2000, he became one of the great religious leaders of the 20th century, a man whose style and beliefs reminded Church historians of one of his storied predecessors, Archbishop John Hughes. Hughes built St. Patrick's Cathedral and the Catholic schools in New

York, and defended his flock from physical assault by nativist Know-Nothings and outright discrimination from Yankee New York. John Hughes was not a man to back down from confrontation. Nor, as the world soon discovered, was John O'Connor.

During his years as Cardinal-Archbishop of New York, John O'Connor's name was attached to several public controversies, most of them concerning abortion and some gay rights issues. Because he believed that life begins at conception, he vigorously opposed abortion, and because he believed that no legislator and certainly no doctor had the power to take away life, he argued against capital punishment and euthanasia. Early on in his tenure in New York, he opposed gay-rights legislation and condom availability in public schools. Once engaged on these issues, there was little doubt where he and the Church stood, and why. He made himself readily accessible (perhaps, he later admitted, a little too accessible) to members of the news media hungry for controversy. In doing so, he became a stock character in the nation's conversation of the 1980s and 1990s—a time of loud voices and cultural change. The role he was assigned was that of a stern, authoritarian upholder of orthodox Catholicism.

That he was—that, and so much more. He supported strikers and lectured business leaders about justice. He kept open Catholic schools in poor, non-Catholic neighborhoods. He visited the sick and dying, and ministered to the grieving. He defended the poor and the handicapped, and he gave hope to the discouraged. This other side of him, the side that his family and co-workers saw, that those to whom he ministered saw, that those he inspired saw, was largely unknown during his life and even now, after his death. The testimony of those who knew him, some for years, others only fleetingly, offers another look at a man so many people thought they knew.

Their stories of inspiration and compassion, faith and wit, show that he is with us still, still preaching, still ministering, still teaching, and still telling the truth as he saw it. He was truly a man full of God's grace.

Family

Each night, my priest secretary gives me a special blessing. That blessing is very meaningful to me ... It is a reminder of a blessing that I received as a child each evening from my father. It was a wonderful custom which prevailed for many years, and it has remained with me.

—Cardinal O'Connor's Sunday homily, Feb. 20, 2000

RARELY DID A DAY PASS without John O'Connor making some reference to his family—his parents, his siblings, his nieces and nephews. As a Roman Catholic priest, he took vows that precluded a family of his own, but those same vows ensured that he would form a family of another sort: the brotherhood of his fellow priests, the kinship of other religious people, the intimate relationships born of faith, suffering, and compassion.

BETTER THAN A COWBOY SUIT

When he was about to turn seven years old, John O'Connor decided he wanted a cowboy suit for his birthday. This was a slight change in little John's priorities—the previous Christmas, he had asked for a pony. His father, Thomas, made the undeniable argument that a row house in Philadelphia was no place for a pony. Christmas came and went—next on the calendar was January 15, John's birthday.

He didn't get the cowboy suit, and resolved to run away from home "as soon as I could save up 15 or 20 cents," he once wrote. Nearly a month passed, and he had just a nickel. When he came home from school on Feb. 10, 1927, John had a surprise waiting for him. The cowboy suit? No, a baby sister named Mary. Despite the seven years between them, John and Mary grew up to be lifelong friends. John introduced Mary to her future husband, Hugh Ward, and together she and Hugh had eight children.

My parents were very spiritual people. We lived some distance from the local church, St. Clement's, but we were brought there for the missions and for religious services. It was always done with love, so it was never something we felt was imposed on us. I remember watching my parents say the Rosary. My parents were true to their religion, and we lived by what we were taught. The doctrines of our faith were sacrosanct.

Even as a kid, my brother was a workaholic. He ran a bicycle repair shop out of the basement. He would be outside the stores to help people who couldn't carry all their groceries home. He also was a telegram delivery boy. He always figured out some way to make a few dollars, which he then turned over to my mother.

As a child, I remember him wanting to be a priest. He would say to me, "Come on, I'll show you how to say Mass." And he'd go through it with me. I believe the first time he mentioned to my parents that he wanted to be a priest, he was 15. Their reaction was, "That's nice. Mention it again in a year, and we'll see." A year later, he told them that he wanted to go into the seminary. The truth is, my parents didn't think he was going to pass the entrance exam. He did, of course. I think the reason they thought he wouldn't pass is that he spent most of his childhood in public school, and only the last couple of years in West Catholic High School.

He taught at St. James High School [in Pennsylvania] for a while, and for years I'd get calls from people telling me how he had saved their lives, that if it hadn't been for him, they'd be in jail.

He introduced me to my husband, Hugh. They were very close friends, and when my husband died in 1983, he became my children's surrogate father. He had a great impact on them. My children say they had three parents, and anytime something happened in the family, it was, "We have to call Uncle Jack." We made great efforts to see him when he was in the Navy. We would pack the kids into the car and off we'd go. My brother would call and say, "I'm in Quantico [the Marine base in Virginia] to do a confirmation," and my husband and I would go down there for the confirmation, have dinner, and drive back. He was so much a part of my life, and there was no place my husband would not have gone for him.

After my father died, if my brother was free for the holidays, he came to my home. He always said grace, and I used to make a particular kind of stuffing for him. It was like what my mother made, and he enjoyed it. On Christmas morning, the children would pile into his bedroom and start saying, "Uncle Jack, Uncle Jack, look at this!" He was like the Pied Piper. He'd take them to the lake to skate on Christmas.

He got a good taste of what it's like to raise children. It was one of the things that made him sensitive to the needs of parents. I had eight children nine years apart, and he spent a good period of time with all of them. He was an imporant part of their lives.

UNCLE JACK

In his biography of Cardinal O'Connor, Nat Hentoff said of Eileen Ward Christian, "She brings cheer when few others can." Mrs. Christian, the Cardinal's niece, is Mary and Hugh Ward's youngest child. She attended law school at St. John's University in New York, and lived in nearby White Plains during most of her uncle's tenure as Cardinal-Archbishop. On August 15, 1998, Uncle Jack presided at the wedding of

Eileen Ward to Jefrey Christian. A year later, the couple re-
ceived a letter from the Cardinal congratulating them on their
first anniversary. It was written the day doctors found a tumor
on his brain.

My first recollection of my uncle was around 1965, when he returned from Vietnam. I would have been three or four years old at the time. It was always a special time when he came to stay with us. My parents would prepare us, and we'd all get excited—it was like having a third parent who was coming home from his tour of duty. He always saw the good in us, because we were always on our best behavior when he was around. He got the liberty of spoiling us, of spending one-on-one time with us.

Whenever he came for a visit, it was known that we all had to get up at some ungodly hour, come downstairs in our pajamas, and we'd have Mass in the living room, with my brothers acting as altar servers and my father as the lector. As a chaplain, my uncle always had a traveling kit with him, so he always had his altar materials with him. His homilies, I remember, were very instructive, whether he was giving them in our living room or later in St. Patrick's Cathedral.

When I was eight and one of my brothers was nine and one of my sisters was 10 —this would have been when Uncle Jack was based in Newport, R.I.,—he had a friend who was a chaplain at the Naval Academy, and he took us to visit him. We got a tour of the place, stayed with his friend, went on canoe trips on the Potomac. He did that for us all the time. When my brother Hugh was in Europe, Uncle Jack took my brother John to visit Hugh there. They all met at Auschwitz and spent a few days touring that area. In retrospect, I realize now that my uncle was trying to expose us to a bigger world outside our little town of Prospect Park, Pennsylvania. But we sort of overtook his life at some points. He must have been thinking, "Where did I get all these kids?"

What a blessing we had in him, though. I spent lots of time with him and other priests, hearing their discussions of spirituality. My understanding of my faith is so much expanded because of what he taught me. I spent a lifetime—until I was 38 years old—listening to his homilies.

I also got to spend a lot of one-on-one time with him, going over every problem I had in my life. He was my own personal spiritual director. Throughout my life I heard from him about his reverence for the Eucharist, and for the Mass, and the meaning behind it all. He explained small things, but they had a great impact. I'm now the local expert on the Mass.

I'm sure the people around him got so sick of hearing about me. [Laughs] I would be at a dinner, and somebody would say, "I know all about you. Your uncle talks about you all the time." And I'm thinking, "Oh, my goodness, what the heck is he saying now!" The people around him, like Maura O'Kelly, the housekeeper, would call and say, "You have to come by. He needs a night off." Or they'd say, "You have to talk him into taking a vacation." But there was nobody who could talk him into taking a vacation. If anybody could try, I would try. But it didn't work.

THE MAN IN A UNIFORM

Hugh Ward was the second of Hugh and Mary Ward's children. He traveled extensively in Europe with his Uncle Jack in the 1970s, and Uncle Jack paid for Hugh's stint as a graduate student in France in 1978. The future Cardinal told friends, "I offered to send him anywhere, and of course, he chose Paris." Hugh shared his uncle's interest in politics and global affairs, and has gone on to become a federal prosecutor in the U.S. Attorney's office in Knoxville, Tenn. He and his wife, Fran, have two children.

In most of the pictures you see of Uncle Jack, he's in flowing robes or in a priest's Roman collar. But in my strongest memories of him, he's wearing a uniform. For the first 27 years of my life, he was in the military, and he was always in a shirt and tie and a uniform. It was a little hard getting used to seeing him in more priestly garb as the years went on.

I remember him going off to Vietnam in 1965 to be with the Marines in Da Nang. He'd send home audiotapes instead of letters, and we'd play them at home. They were pretty businesslike. I think he was trying to calm the fears of my grandmother. We knew he was in a combat zone, and we knew he was living out of a tent, so we were keenly aware of the danger he was in—we were on pins and needles the whole time. But after he returned, we never really spoke about his Vietnam experience. I remember reading about it, many years later, in a story printed after he became a Cardinal. He told a reporter a story about being in a helicopter that came under fire. He was a smoker then, and he was smoking a cigar. At some point, he threw the cigar out the chopper and he vowed to God that if he survived this incident, he would stop smoking. He did, and he did.

UNCLE JACK'S ROOMMATE

Joanne Ward Mohrmann was Hugh and Mary Ward's third child. Irreverent and candid, she delights in telling stories showing the human side of Uncle Jack, the side she saw when she went to live with him at the Naval Academy in the early 1970s. She and her husband, Jeff, now live in Manitou Springs, Col. They have four children.

Living with him was very adventurous. [Laughs] It was 1972. I was 17 when I got there, just out of high school. He was the first Catholic senior chaplain at the Naval Academy, and he had this big house with seven bedrooms. So my parents said, "Go live with Uncle Jack and go to college down there." I always felt they were trying to get me away from my high school boyfriend. [Laughs]

I lived with Uncle Jack from the time I was 17 until I was 21. He would explain things to me a little bit differently than my parents did. Or he would encourage me to find things out for myself. I would get angry sometimes at my parents—I remember once I was mad with them over something they were doing with one of my brothers. I was complaining to Uncle Jack, you know, saying, "Why do they do that?" And he said, "Well, gee, honey, if you want to know, why don't you ask them?" So I went and asked them, and they gave me a perfectly logical explanation.

On other matters, he was very much like a parent. I was 17, living on a campus with 4,200 men—there were no women in the Naval Academy at the time. So he'd say things like, "You're staying out too late." We fought about the things a teenager and a parent would fight about. But he did teach me how to cook—he often would have 50 or 60 people over for dinner, and at 18 years old, I was cooking for that many people. And he was teaching me how to do it. What I found amazing is that he knew how to do that, too.

I took care of his military uniforms while I lived with him. One time he asked me if I would pick up his uniforms from the cleaners, and I forgot. When I came home that night, he asked me where his clothes were, and I told him, "I forgot." And he said to me, "Joanne, if it was important to you, you wouldn't have forgotten. Apparently, the fact that I needed them wasn't important enough for you to remember." I never forgot anything again for him, but now that I've gone on in life, when I ask my kids to do something, or my husband, and they forget, I have that same instant reaction: It wasn't important to you. Sometimes, I don't think that was a good thing for him to say to me.

He was a perfectionist, and he wanted things done properly. I remember when I was sharing this gigantic house with him, with a big winding staircase, he was standing at the bottom, complaining to me about one of his particular white uniforms, and I was at the top, and I threw the uniform all the way down to him and said, "Clean it yourself. I can't do any better!" [Laughs] Still, he was a very loving uncle.

Living with him—let's see if I can phrase this right—was almost like living with somebody who was constantly counseling. He would be very careful not to do anything that would alienate you, which is probably pretty normal for a parent, and at the same time, he was trying to lead you constantly in the right direction. He was very good and very successful at it. I did get rid of the high school boyfriend, I did graduate from college, and he was very happy when I chose the man I married. And he was happy that I hadn't completely screwed up my life by the time I was 25. [Laughs]

THE SILENT TREATMENT

Hugh Ward

I lived with my uncle and my sister for a while when he was at the Naval Academy. He helped find me a job as a mail clerk in the House of Representatives. I think we got a chance to expose him to what it's like to raise teenagers. He loaned me his car once, and I took it and didn't come home until the next day. He never asked me where I was, and I never told him, but he reacted in typical Uncle Jack fashion: days of the silent treatment. Then it reached the boiling point, and we thrashed it out, and it blew over. He was like a parent, in every sense of the word. In fact, my sister Eileen used to send him cards on Father's Day.

HE PICKED THE DATE

Joanne Mohrmann

When I left Washington in 1979, he was Chief of Chaplains and still living there. I took a job in New York, and I was probably there two months when he called me—from New York—and told me to meet him someplace. And I showed up, and that's when Cardinal Cooke made the announcement that my uncle was going to become a bishop in charge of the [Catholic Church's] military vicariate. So now he was going to move to New York full time.

I met Jeff, my husband, while I was in New York, and we'd occasionally go to see Uncle Jack at Mass. When we decided to get married, the first thing I wanted to do, even before we told our parents, was to tell Uncle Jack. I knew, knowing Uncle Jack for so many years, that he was going to require us to take premarital instruction with him, and that he was going to pick a date for the wedding—that would not be up to me, because he was going to do the wedding. I kept calling him, but he was traveling a lot, so I finally called his secretary and said, "Make me an appointment." Finally, we went in one evening to see him, and we told him we wanted to get married. And he said, "Oh, let me look on my calendar." Sure enough, he sat there and picked out the date of my wedding. Then he lined up the premarital instructions, when they were going to start, and then he took us out to dinner.

I was out walking with him one day in New York, and we're getting ready to go into the subway. We see this huge man dressed as a woman, asking for money. And, you know, I was a hardened New Yorker. I was going to walk right by that guy. But Uncle Jack didn't walk by that guy. Uncle Jack stood there and talked and reached into his pocket and gave him everything he had. I know he did because later, when we went for ice cream, he didn't have any money and I had to pay. Of course, the most he ever carried in his pocket was three cents. [Laughs]

PRE-CANA FROM UNCLE JACK

Hugh Ward

I was offered a job in New York City in 1988 and I took it. I thought it would be nice to have a chance to see my uncle again regularly. I met my wife, Fran, on a blind date, and eventually introduced her to my uncle—it was sort of a rite of passage. She was not Catholic, but he never said to me, "I have a problem here." When we decided to get married, he gave us our pre-Cana instructions, which turned out to be interesting. We got to the section on birth control, and he wanted to let Fran know the Church's position on the subject. Fran was just finishing her residency as a surgeon, so she was just getting off the ground. He asked her directly: "How do you feel about artificial contraception?" Now, we knew we were going to have to confront this issue, and Fran got advice from people who said, "Everybody just lies to the priest about these things." But Fran said, "I'm not going to lie to him." So she told him, "Look, I could make up a story, but I have to be totally honest with you. We're probably going to have to do this thing [use artificial contraception] until we get our feet on the ground."

My uncle would never try to impose anything on her, but he turned to me and said, "How do you feel?" And I said, "Well, I kind of agree." And he said, "Well, I can't participate in marrying you then. I'm not telling you that you can't get married, but I can't be the priest who will do the ceremony." That broke all of our hearts. We went back and forth for a couple of weeks—we weren't angry, we were just trying to get through it. We decided to be counseled by a natural family planner from the archdiocese. And, in the end, Uncle Jack married us in the Lady Chapel in St. Patrick's Cathedral.

ANYONE FOR TENNIS?

Joanne Mohrmann

In 1990, my husband became a Catholic. He had always come to Mass—that was a big thing for us. When he started taking classes in preparation for his conversion, he told people he got the accelerated course because of my uncle. Uncle Jack came out to Colorado that summer and did a big thing in our little church for my husband. Now, our church is tiny, with about 80 families. But in the summertime, lots of tourists come to church. So, when Jeff became a Catholic, it was done during a regular Sunday Mass in the summer with a church full of tourists. And the lector gets up there and announces, "Our celebrant today will be John Cardinal O'Connor, the Archbishop of New York." These people start looking at each other—they were thinking, "We went to this little tiny town in Colorado, and Cardinal O'Connor is showing up?"

Family 23

We used to vacation in the Poconos regularly, and Uncle Jack came along. Even as recently as 1998, after Eileen [her sister] got married, we all congregated in the Poconos, near Lake Wallenpaupack. That time, Uncle Jack got in the canoe with me and fell out. [Laughs] That was pretty funny—he was OK, he was just wet.

We were in the Poconos sometime in the late 1980s. Uncle Jack was already the Archbishop of New York. One day, Eileen and I decided we were going to go play tennis. And Uncle Jack said, "Well, I want to go." So he went into another room to change his clothes for tennis. And he came out in a pair of regular black shoes, black socks, a yellow golf shirt, and a pair of shorts that Eileen and I swore were his boxers. We don't think anything of it—the guy doesn't have any tennis clothes, apparently, and it's just Eileen and I. We're family, what do we care? So we go out and play tennis and after a while this very young couple pulls into the parking lot. They want to play next.

So we finish playing and we're getting ready to walk off and this young man gets out of his car and walks over to Uncle Jack and says, "Excuse me, are you Archbishop O'Connor?" Eileen and I are just standing there mortified, and we're saying, "Say no. Say no. Please say no. Please lie. Do not tell anybody who you are." He looked ridiculous! And he said, "Yes!" [Laughs] So he stood there and chitchatted with this guy looking to us like he was standing in his underwear. [Laughs] And that year we all bought him tennis clothes for Christmas. We said, "Uncle Jack, we're never going out on a tennis court again with you unless you wear these tennis shoes and these tennis outfits." Knowing him, he probably gave it all away.

Ministry

I am so happy to be a priest I can't imagine not being one.
—from Cardinal O'Connor's column in
Catholic New York

THE CALL TO PRIESTHOOD took John O'Connor from the streets of Philadelphia to the quiet halls of St. Charles Borromeo Seminary; from the battlefields of Vietnam to the classrooms of the Naval Academy; from St. Peter's Cathedral in Scranton, Pennsylvania, to St. Patrick's Cathedral in midtown Manhattan. He performed many roles: administrator, bureaucrat, politician, boss, Prince of the Church. But always and everywhere, he was a priest, performing work he felt he was born to do, caring for the sick, counseling those in need, advising the clergy, and administering the sacraments.

"WE WILL PREVAIL"

The Rev. J.C. Williams is a Baptist minister from Georgia who met John O'Connor when the two men were Navy chaplains in the 1960s. When O'Connor became Chief of Chaplains and a Rear Admiral in the early 1970s, he remembered his friend J.C. Williams. The Naval Academy needed a new chaplain; Rear Admiral O'Connor recommended just one candidate for the job, rather than the traditional three: J.C. Williams, who thus became the first African-American chaplain at Annapolis. Asked if he was surprised to watch his friend's rise to prominence, Rev. Williams said: "The only thing that surprised me about Father O'Connor was that he didn't become Pope."

In the Navy, Roman Catholic chaplains traditionally did not have many administrative roles because they had such heavy liturgical responsibilities. John O'Connor broke that mold. He was an administrative genius. He knew how to get things done in a military system, which I saw when I was appointed to the Naval Academy.

It started a year before I actually got there, when Father O'Connor first told me that I would be going to the Academy. He asked me not to discuss his intentions with anybody. "We will prevail," he said. That was the kind of strength he exuded.

A year went by, during which I was out of the country, in

Diego Garcia with the SeaBees [the Navy's Construction Brigade]. All during that time, I was getting confidential letters from Father O'Connor telling me to prepare to go to the Naval Academy. When the time came, I had to reveal this to my commanding officer, and he said, "Well, you'll have to tell Father O'Connor that you can't go." It was awkward timing, because I was the only Protestant chaplain on the island. So I sent him a letter telling him I couldn't go. I suggested a time that would be convenient. A telegram came back and said simply, "You will be on the next plane off that island." So, I was on the next plane off that island.

When I first came on active duty in 1969, there were only three African-American chaplains in the Navy. Nobody had been more forthright about the need for bringing in more priests than Father O'Connor, and he tied the need for more African-American chaplains with the need for more Roman Catholic priests. Eventually, we raised the number of African-American chaplains in the Navy to 80. It was Father O'Connor who said we could do it, and it was Father O'Connor who convinced people in the Navy to open the purse strings to make it happen.

He often invited my wife and me to his home for social events that would be crowded with dignitaries and foreign chaplains. He was a gracious host, effortless and always correct. But when he was hosting something, there was always a reason. You weren't there just for fun. [Laughs] When we'd get an invitation, my wife and I would say, "OK, what's the agenda?" There was always something going on at those events, and the people in the room generally didn't know it.

He was a hard taskmaster to work for. Some said he was intimidating, but no, he was just so driven by where he wanted to go, and he had a sense of destiny that reminded him he didn't have all the time in the world to get there. I served on about half a dozen promotion boards with him. We'd have to explain our decision in writing, and sometimes we'd be working on the document until midnight, and Father O'Connor would say, "Give it to me." He'd have it done in minutes.

If you worked for him, you walked away saying, "Well, I can work for just about anybody now."

CHIEF OF CHAPLAINS

Admiral James Watkins was Chief of Naval Operations under President Ronald Reagan from 1982 to 1986. He met then-Monsignor O'Connor in 1975, when they were based in Washington. Later, in the early 1980s, O'Connor consulted the admiral when the U.S. Bishops Conference was writing a pastoral letter on nuclear arms. And in 1987, the admiral and the Cardinal served on President Reagan's AIDS commission, which the admiral chaired. They jointly sponsored an annual pilgimage to the Maryland home of Saint Elizabeth Ann Seton, whose two sons had served in the U.S. Navy.

I first met him when I became chief of naval personnel in the spring of 1975. At that time he was Monsignor O'Connor and was chief of chaplains for the U.S. Navy, with the rank of Rear Admiral. I was Vice Admiral at the time, and he was one of the officers in my purview. I had a lineup every morning at 9 o'clock, and I brought in all the top assistants. Admiral O'Connor was one of those in these meetings, and we always had a good back and forth because, if you know John O'Connor, you know he didn't hesitate to make his views well known. We used to have some nice exchanges, and I once said to him, "Well, what you're telling me is if I don't do what you want, I'm going to be excommunicated." [Laughs] And, of course, he comes back with some snide comment. [Laughs again]

We did some pretty important things. We established what I called Family Service Centers, which had never existed before. When we moved to an all-voluntary military [in the 1970s], it was extremely important that we be competitive with industry and business. We needed desperately to get into the modern world of how to deal with families. The Family Service Centers included places where chaplains could go in search of their flock, so to speak. John O'Connor was a big part of that.

He was a brilliant homilist. When he was Chief of Chaplains, he went out and taught his chaplains how to preach. This was for all denominations. He said, "You have to start a week ahead of time, get your thoughts together, do a thorough review of what's coming up in the Scripture, and do your job right. Don't wing it. People want to listen to you." That's the way he was. He was a teacher to his chaplains.

BISHOP OF SCRANTON

Mary Ellen Keating was a well-known television anchor-woman and reporter at the CBS affiliate in Scranton in 1983 when John O'Connor was appointed the new bishop of the Diocese of Scranton. Before he took up his new post, Ms. Keating arranged to interview Bishop O'Connor in Manhattan, where he was serving as head of the Catholic Church's military vicariate. "I just hit it off with him right away," she said. Before long, she was working for him in the newly created position of executive director of communications for the diocese. She is now director of corporate communications for Barnes & Noble.

The day before his installation as Bishop of Scranton, there was a special Mass in St. Peter's Cathedral. There was a long procession going into the Cathedral, and I was outside, covering it for the station. As he passed by, he saw me and said, "Mary Ellen, if you can't get a seat inside, I know somebody who might be able to help you." It was remarks like that which always brightened somebody's day.

I regularly attended Mass in St. Peter's, and one day, as he was outside greeting people, he took me aside and said, "I have a proposition for you. Please schedule some time to see me this week." I was curious about this, but I had no idea what he had in mind. I went to see him about a week later, and he said, "You know, I've been impressed with your work, and I think we could work together." He said there was a need for a communications effort in the diocese, and he thought I could help him. "Now, I can't pay you a lot of money," he said, "but I want you to think it over."

I talked to a lot of people who didn't think I should leave my career. I had worked in TV for a while, and was a local personality. People thought I was crazy to think about walking away from my career for a job that actually didn't exist. Even my family was opposed to it.

I took time to think about it, and I wound up surprising myself. I decided, somehow, that this was a once in a lifetime opportunity. I realized that I was never going to meet somebody like this again. I just had to take the chance. It's hard to explain. I did what nobody thought I should do. I left my job to go to work for him.

Never before had a lay person been given such an important position in the diocese, never mind a woman. He was a real pioneer in the diocese in that regard. As the executive director for communications, I went to weekly meetings with the diocese staff, 99 percent of whom wore black suits and white Roman collars. There was myself and a nun who were at those meetings—everybody else was a priest. And those meetings were run like a business, which was something new for everybody. They started on time, and you were expected to be on time, too. There was an agenda, and you had to be prepared to offer something because you knew you'd be asked. You couldn't just sit there like a bump on a log. He demanded the best from people, and because of the kind of person he was, people were willing to give it. He was a whirlwind. You never simply went home at 5 o'clock. You went to the rectory, had a working dinner with him, and then worked well into the evening. That's the way he was. But I never was tired, and I never complained. It was just so great to have a chance to work with a man like that.

I remember the day he told me that he was leaving. I knew in advance, because I had to help prepare the announcement [in January, 1984]. I went into his office and he said to me, "This is the hardest thing I'll ever have to tell you. The Holy Father has asked me to become Archbishop of New York." He was very sad about it, because he loved the work he was doing in the diocese, and he had been there only eight or nine months.

A PREMONITION

Mary Ward

After [New York Archbishop Terence] Cardinal Cooke died, my husband insisted that my brother was going to be named to New York. Cardinal Cooke died on the sixth of October, 1983, and Hugh said to my brother, "You're going to New York." And my brother said, "I just got to Scranton, and there's no way I'll be taken away after such a short time." Hugh died on the 31st of October, so he never knew that he was right all along. When my brother called me to tell me he was going to New York, I laughed and said, "Hugh is up there tugging on God's arm, saying, 'Send him to New York. Send him to New York.' And God said, 'All right, already, I'll do it. Now leave me alone!'"

I once told my brother that the reason I liked Scranton better than New York is that I always had a place to park in Scranton.

A POUNDING ON THE DOOR

Monsignor Peter Finn, rector of St. Joseph's Seminary in Dunwoodie, N.Y., was director of communications for the New York Archdiocese under Cardinal Cooke. He continued in that post for several years under Cardinal O'Connor before serving as pastor of St. Joseph-St. Thomas Church on Staten Island.

The morning before Bishop O'Connor was to be announced as the new Archbishop of New York, I went up to Scranton by bus, joined by Gerry Costello [then editor of *Catholic New York*, the archdiocesan newspaper]. We stayed that evening in a motel, and at 5 o'clock in the morning, there was a pounding on the door. It was Gerry Costello. He had just gotten a call from Bishop O'Connor, who wanted us to come over for breakfast. I threw on some clothes and went to the rectory. Bishop O'Connor came downstairs, dressed in black pants and a white shirt, and proceeded to make coffee and pour orange juice for us. I was taken by the fact that he was so casual. He was really disarming—that was his charm. Geez, and a few hours later I was concelebrating Mass with him, the new Archbishop of New York.

NEW MAN IN TOWN

When John O'Connor was appointed to the Archdiocese of New York, Monsignor Thomas Bergin was the principal of Monsignor Farrell High School on Staten Island. In his younger days as Farrell's last Latin teacher, Monsignor Bergin wore a slightly rebellious red beard and, on sunny days, he protected his fair complexion with a pith helmet. The beard and the helmet were gone by March 19, 1984, as he helped usher people to pews in St. Patrick's Cathedral for the installation Mass of the new Archbishop. "As I heard him speak, with his wit and his intelligence, I knew we were into something very different," Monsignor Bergin said. "I thought to myself, 'Boy, this is going to be some ride.'" In 1992, Cardinal O'Connor appointed Monsignor Bergin as vicar of education for the archdiocese, and, some time later, added to the monsignor's duties by naming him Chancellor of the Archdiocese. Monsignor Bergin moved into the Cardinal's residence, and from that vantage point, he watched, prayed with, and worked for "the most intelligent man I ever met, and the toughest boss I ever worked for."

One of the first things Cardinal O'Connor said he'd do is visit all 19 of the vicariates [a geographical subdivision within the archdiocese]. And in April of 1984 we found out that Staten Island was going to be first such visit. A bunch of us were put in charge of making the arrangements for a whirlwind tour. O'Connor came over on the ferry from

Manhattan, and we borrowed a car from the custodian at Farrell [High School] to take him around. It was a big white Chevy—nothing fancy. It was one helluva tour. I remember picking him up in the morning after the first day—he was staying at the rectory at Blessed Sacrament with [Bishop] Paddy Ahearn—and as we walked in, he was in the kitchen in black pants and a white shirt, pouring cornflakes into a bowl. He said, "I'm used to rectory living." He looked just like the parish priest you grew up with, which is what he was.

What impressed me during this tour is that he had the high school kids eating out of his hands. And what was even more amazing, he never used notes, and he never gave the same talk twice. I watched this and thought, "My God, this is an extraordinary man." Near the end of the tour, we stopped the car at Resurrection Cemetery [an archdiocesan facility on Staten Island]. O'Connor said, "OK, it's picture time." And he posed with all of us individually. That's a picture I treasure. I'm not a kiss-up, but I really was taken with this guy.

The Holy Spirit certainly works in its own way. Spelly [Francis Cardinal Spellman] was a great builder—a man for his times. Cardinal Cooke was a reserved man, and he worked behind the scenes and consolidated. He was a man for his times. And John O'Connor was never afraid to stand up to anything. A man for his times, again.

ST. PATRICK'S DAY

It's tempting to describe Republican Congressman Peter King of Long Island as the political world's equivalent of Cardinal O'Connor. Like the Cardinal, the Congressman is pro-life and conservative on most cultural issues. And like the Cardinal, he is a strong supporter of organized labor. Congressman King met the Cardinal in 1985, when Mr. King was chosen as grand marshal of the St. Patrick's Day Parade in New York. The occasion offered the new archbishop a glimpse of the roiling politics of his global archdiocese. The selection of Mr. King, then the Nassau County Comptroller, prompted the Irish government to boycott the parade because of Mr. King's friendship with Gerry Adams and his Sinn Fein party in Northern Ireland, who, as the political representatives of the IRA, were pariahs at the time. The Archbishop came under great pressure from the Irish and British governments to join the boycott.

About 10 days before the parade—it was late in the afternoon on a Thursday—I went to the archdiocesan headquarters on First Avenue for a meeting with the Archbishop. There was a real question whether or not he would review the parade. I went up to the top floor and was shown to a waiting room while the Archbishop finished up another appointment. I felt like a little kid waiting to see the principal. I remember it was very dark up there in that room.

When I was called to his office, he was very businesslike. Not antagonistic, just businesslike. He told me that he had been told that I was planning to have IRA supporters in the parade. He told me that if I tried to do anything that would disrupt the parade, he'd order it moved over to Lexington Avenue (two blocks away from the Cathedral). Of course, I wasn't planning anything of the sort. And then he asked me to tell him why he should review the parade. He listened to me, and told me that he would be watching events carefully.

Then, the night before the parade, I was at the annual Friendly Sons of St. Patrick's dinner. I saw the Archbishop on the dais, sitting near [then-Senator] Alfonse D'Amato. I went over to say hello, and all of a sudden D'Amato starts making jokes about the controversy. "That's all I need now," I thought. The Archbishop smiled when he saw me, and then he said, "If you walk up Fifth Avenue on your knees, that still wouldn't repay me for all the anguish you've caused me." What I learned later is that the Irish and British governments really put the pressure on to boycott the parade, and what they learned is that the Archbishop wasn't somebody you tried to push around. He didn't join the boycott.

The next day, after the annual St. Patrick's Day Mass in the Cathedral, my family posed for pictures with the Archbishop. At the time, my daughter had her arm in a splint because of a gymnastics injury. O'Connor looks at her and says, "What happened to you? Did you get involved in one of your father's causes?"

A SOFT VOICE

Jennifer Lynch went to work for the Inner City Scholarship Fund in the mid-1990s. The fund is administered by the Archdiocese's Development Office, and raises money to give scholarships to poor urban children so they can attend Catholic school. Many scholarship winners are not Catholic; Cardinal O'Connor was determined to keep a Catholic school presence in poor neighborhoods that many white Catholics had left in the 1950s and '60s. In many such communities, the local Catholic school is an oasis, offering the potential for salvation from poverty and fear. Ms. Lynch now works for VH 1's Save the Music Foundation, which seeks to restore music programs in public schools.

The Inner City Scholarship Fund was my first job in the nonprofit sector. I was put in charge of events in the Cardinal's residence. My first one was an event for Japanese businessmen who donated $1,000 each to the Scholarship Fund. [Former New York Mayor] Ed Koch was the master of ceremonies.

So this is my first big event. I arranged for a podium and a microphone. The night arrives, and I get to the Cardinal's residence [behind St. Patrick's Cathedral] to make sure everything is set up. I see there's a podium, and the microphone is there, so I figure we're good to go. With about 20 minutes to go before people were due to arrive, I checked the mike and I realize there's no sound system. That's because I didn't ask for one! And now it's too late, and I'm totally distraught. I now have to explain to His Eminence that there's no sound system. So I went over to him and explained that he'd simply have to project so people could hear him. He listened, then he put his hand on my shoulder and said, "But young lady, I don't like to raise my voice." I realized later how true that was. There are two kinds of leaders: There's the leader who takes charge of a room and speaks out and you can't help but listen. Like Ed Koch. And then there are the leaders who speak quietly, who draw you in. You lean into them. That's what Cardinal O'Connor was like.

A UTILITY INFIELDER

Cardinal O'Connor shattered many a glass ceiling with his appointments of women to positions formerly held exclusively by men. Even still, Eileen White was exceptional: She was young, a lawyer, a lay person, and she was given a position of authority in a job that didn't exist before her. After passing the bar exam, she put aside her ambition to be a prosecutor to work at what she thought would be a temporary job in the Cardinal's office. "My title was special counsel," Ms. White said, "but the Cardinal liked to describe me as his utility in-fielder." Utility infielders, however, generally are not called upon as often as Ms. White was during a tenure that spanned from her youth to the beginning of middle age. A graduate of the College of the Holy Cross in Worcester, Mass., and St. John's University Law School, Ms. White is now at the investment firm of Goldman, Sachs.

Through Eileen Ward [the Cardinal's niece], I got to know the Cardinal during my second year of law school. We had dinner with him a couple of times and went to Midnight Mass and then to the residence in 1984. We got to be fast friends—we had an instant rapport. He had a great sense of humor, and I like to think I have a great sense of humor, too. When I was finishing law school, I wanted to be a prosecutor in the district attorney's office. The Cardinal said, "Come and work with me for three months, and after that, you can figure out what you want to do next." He talked about the possibility that I'd go to work with Catholic Charities as a lawyer. I said to myself, well, three months is reasonable. So I took the bar exam, and started with the Cardinal in December, 1986. Thirteen years later, I was still with him.

He'd often say, "I'm from a little row house in Philadelphia. That's who I am." Kings, queens, heads of states—it didn't matter. He knew who he was, and was very comfortable with that. When he met a wealthy couple [at a fundraising event], he was more likely to be concerned about whether their marriage was intact, how the children were, and whether they were in good standing with the Church. That was more important to him than how many millions they had.

He was very much absorbed in his role as Archbishop, and when we had down time, more often than not, the conversation was about an issue of the day, or something the Holy Father had asked him to do. Generally, he didn't indulge in frivolous conversation, although there were moments when we talked about golf. I played with him a couple of times early in his tenure—he told me I was his first real golf coach. He played every August at a reunion of his seminary class. Oh, he loved golf. When he was a Navy chaplain in Washington, he'd get on the course at 6 in the morning, play nine holes, and be at his desk at 8 A.M. He loved baseball, too, but he lost patience with professional sports, with the amounts of money the players were making, and the way they conducted themselves. He stopped following sports, although occasionally on a Sunday, we'd be working on some matter and the golf tournament would be on television.

HIS HONOR, THE MAYOR

Ed Koch was halfway through his memorable 12 years as Mayor of New York when John O'Connor arrived as Archbishop. The two men quickly formed one of the most remarkable friendships in 20th-century New York. They shared meals together, wrote a book together (His Eminence and His Honor), comforted each other and teased each other publicly. And they sued each other several times over church-state issues. Through it all, there was no mistaking their mutual affection, but the public saw only a hint of the seemingly unlikely intimacy they shared, this outspoken voice of Catholic dogma and this Jewish politician from Greenwich Village.

We hit it off right away in part because I made it very clear, and he must have been told by his associates, that I supported the social services the archdiocese provided under contract with the city. There are many people in government, then and now, who believe that services should be nonsectarian in terms of their delivery. But I had concluded early on that the archdiocese had led the way in so many areas, and it would be ridiculous not to use them. I took the position that people who were associated with the Church delivered services because they believe, as I believe, that you have an obligation to serve your fellow human beings as best you can.

So I fought the battle to make sure the Church was not discriminated against. There was one situation when a deputy commissioner in the Human Resources Administration had written in her own hand a note which said something like, "Go get 'em!" The inference was clear—it was directed with hostility at a Catholic agency providing services. As so often happens, stupidity or God provided that the offending message was sent in error to the Church. [Laughs] So they had it, and they showed it to me. I was mortified. I called in the deputy commissioner and I said, "This is your last chance. Everybody makes mistakes, and I'm sure you're not an evil person, but I want you to know this adminstration wants the help of the clergy. There will not be a second chance." I think the archdiocese appreciated that.

We proposed legislation in 1986 that would prohibit discrimination against gays in housing and employment. The Cardinal was opposed to it, but we defeated him. In later years, I tried to negotiate a compromise to get a hearing on a partial birth abortion ban in New York in exchange for getting a hearing on a state gay rights bill. I called the Cardinal, and he said, "That's fair. I support that." And he said, "I don't oppose barring discrimination based on sexual orientation with respect to employment and housing." His position was, condemn the sin, love the sinner.

REVIEW OF THE TROOPS

Cardinal O'Connor named Sister Joan Curtin as the first woman director of the Catechetical Office—formerly known as the Confraternity of Christian Doctrine (CCD)—of the New York Archdiocese. From her corner office at the Catholic Center in Manhattan, Sister Joan oversees religious education in the archdiocese's 413 parishes. She is a member of the Congregation of Notre Dame.

I think in the beginning, I had the sense from some sisters that he thought of us as the troops, and he'd deploy us here and there. And it doesn't work like that. We [religious orders] have our own government and authority structure. That was a bit of a problem in the beginning. But I always felt he respected me.

He met with heads of about 35 offices once a week, on Monday, 9:30 to 10:30, rain, shine, sleet, or snow. We sat at a big table and passed a microphone around, and you could say whatever you want. It was a tremendous opportunity to bring to his attention some problem, some event that was occurring, and you know, he never missed a beat. He read everything. He would say to somebody, "You know, three weeks ago I got a letter from you about X. Has that been worked on?" I called it "the review of the troops." I'm sure they must have done something like that in the Navy. [Laughs]

But you know what it did? It connected you to your colleagues. You were able to network with people, and you got to see your colleagues and learn to respect them. That's how he was—he was the Admiral. He didn't take no for an answer when he really wanted something. He would say, "Look, find out how to do it." Dealing with him reminded me of that line from the movie *Apollo 13*, where somebody says, "Failure is not an option." Same thing. [Laughs] And it's wonderful—it's a great challenge.

MONEY MATTERS

Monsignor Charles Kavanagh was vicar for development under Cardinal O'Connor from 1994 to 2000. In that position, the monsignor not only helped to promote the archdiocese and its programs, like the Inner City Scholarship Fund, but he had the unenviable task of arranging meetings between the Cardinal and potential donors. His position existed, he confessed, so that when the time came to make a pitch to wealthy people, Cardinal O'Connor could demur and refer the potential patrons to somebody else. Somebody like Monsignor Kavanagh.

The Cardinal did not like asking people for financial help. In fact, he wouldn't ask. In my position with the development office, I'd bring somebody in for a breakfast with him, a major figure in the New York corporate scene, and the first thing he'd say is: "I don't want your money. I want your advice." [Laughs] And so it was up to me to say, "Well, maybe this person will give both."

He was so reticent about asking for money because in his family, people shared what they could without being asked. He would have a meeting with some potential donor, and that person might ask, "How can I help?" The Cardinal would tell that person to see me, or my predecessor, Bishop Patrick Ahearn.

There was a part of him that was much more comfortable with a poor person. After meeting with a group of Wall Street executives, he would shake his head and say, "I hope my sainted father saw me. We were union people who lived on the other side of the tracks." He was very loyal to his background, and so he was uncomfortable with all the trappings of being a Cardinal. People would come to the residence for a reception and they'd comment how nice the place was, and he'd say, "Well, I'm just a tenant here." He often said, "If my father and mother ever saw me, living at the corner of 50th Street and Madison Avenue . . ." There was an awareness on his part of who he was and how he was raised. This was a great strength, because he was never overwhelmed by all the hoopla.

A STUPID THING

Father Andrew Greeley's novels caused a stir when they first began appearing in the 1980s. Suffice to say, the idea of a priest writing fiction with some sexual content was controversial.

There was an an attempt in Rome to crack down on my novel-writing as inappropriate. They set up a committee, and got word to Cardinal Joseph Bernadin (Father Greeley's bishop). When he told Cardinal O'Connor about it, O'Connor said, "That's a stupid thing. They shouldn't do that." He wrote a letter to Rome about it, and whether or not it was decisive, I don't know. But it never happened.

I never met Cardinal O'Connor. I saw him once from a distance while I was waiting for a cab. He walked by, but we didn't meet. So his support was very generous. Maybe he also had a thought that if the ban had come down, it would have made my publisher's day. [Laughs]

INNER STRENGTH

Joseph Zwilling joined the communications staff of the Archdiocese of New York in the early 1980s. His plan was to stay a year, but he was asked to remain on staff a little longer. A few months later, the archdiocese announced that Terence Cardinal

Cooke was dying of luekemia. "Obviously," he said, "I couldn't leave during that time." Cardinal Cooke, a shy man who avoided the spotlight, died in October, 1983. His replacement was Bishop John O'Connor of Scranton, Pennsylvania. "Suddenly this office was bursting with activity," he said. "I said to myself, 'I can't leave!'" In 1990, Cardinal O'Connor appointed him the archdiocese's new director of communications. Mr. Zwilling was a layman, the first to hold that important position—and he was just 31 years old.

On a bookcase in his corner office at the archdiocese's headquarters are two baseball caps, one with the New York Yankees logo, the other with the Mets. The Yankee hat Archbishop O'Connor put on, to great laughter, during his solemn installation Mass in 1984. The Met hat he put on a day later, in the interests of diplomacy.

The Cardinal was a natural communicator. Shortly after he arrived here, he was scheduled to record a Labor Day message that would be sent to radio stations as a public service announcement. He took off his watch and asked me what I needed. And I said I needed a minute, well, actually 57 seconds, with his thoughts about Labor Day. He said OK, and he put the watch down on the table where he could see it, waited until the second hand hit 12, and started speaking. Fifty-seven seconds later, he was done. And he looks at me and says, "Was that OK? Can I go now?" It was remarkable.

The columns he wrote in *Catholic New York* [the archdiocese's weekly newspaper] were written in longhand drafts. He would bring them in, or if he were away he'd fax them in, with no crossouts. It just flowed out of him. He would edit them later, but 98 percent of what was in that longhand draft was what appeared in the newspaper.

There was something about him—he didn't sleep, he was constantly on the go, and he had this great inner strength. That's why he was Cardinal-Archbishop of New York, and I won't be. [Laughs] Part of me thinks that from the day he got here, he realized that he had only X number of days as Archbishop of New York, and he was going to make the most out of every day that he could. If that meant not doing the paperwork and administrative duties until two in the morning, that's what it meant.

UNDER HOUSE ARREST

Monsignor Bergin

On March 15, 1992—I remember the date exactly—he called me from his car and asked to see me. I figured he was going to ask me to be vicar of education. I loved what I was doing on Staten Island, so I had mixed feelings. I went up to the residence to see him. He asked me to be vicar, and I agreed immediately. I'm from an age when you do what you're told. I was ordained in 1961, before Vatican Council II, and back then, you'd get a letter saying that you were assigned to such and such a parish and that you were to report by Saturday to hear confessions. These days, there's more consulations, and guys have choices.

Then, on January 15, 1993, he asked me if I would be chancellor, which in the New York Archdiocese is the chief financial officer. I agreed to do it, and he said, "OK, on January 15, 1993, on my birthday and the birthday of Dr. Martin Luther King Jr., I hereby appoint you Chancellor of the Archdiocese. But you have to move here." Now I was under house arrest. [Laughs]

When you live in the residence, you're always aware of the history of that old building. I used this big old bathroom with huge ceilings, the kind that never warms up. You freeze when you step out of the shower. The routine of the house was this: All the priests in the house, the priest-secretaries and the vicars, had morning prayers together with the Cardinal. You got your tail in that chapel by 10 after 7. The Cardinal would have been there before that, making his holy hour. After prayers, he'd go to the Cathedral to say 7:30 Mass, which we would concelebrate together. Then we had breakfast at 8 o'-clock and got a lot of business done. And then we'd go over to the Catholic Center [at 1011 First Avenue] for a day's work.

While I was chancellor, I traveled a lot with him. The routine in the car was that he'd always sit in the front seat. He was always the guy from Phildelaphia who would have felt funny sitting in the back. He'd have different colored folders with him, and the custom was you didn't speak unless he spoke to you. I'd sit right behind him, like I was hiding, because I had work to do, too. He'd ask a question, but he couldn't turn all the way around to look at you. And sometimes he'd doze for a while, because this guy just didn't sleep at night—three hours, maybe. But then we'd get to the meeting, and he'd come alive. If it was a public meeting of some sort, the crowds really gave him energy. And he was always fully prepared, and had all the facts and figures at his fingertips.

I'd stay in the back of the hall or auditorium because if somebody asked a wacko question, like why can't we get a high school in such and such a county, when we knew the county couldn't support it, he'd say, "Well, the vicar of education is here somewhere, probably in the back of the hall." He'd have a twinkle in his eye as he said it. And by being in the back of the hall, at least I could think of something as I walked to the front to give an answer.

After the meeting, we were tired, but he'd come to life. He'd be chatting the whole way home, saying, "That lady had a good point about the schools. Look into it." Then he'd get on the telephone in the car and start calling sick priests. He'd say, "Hello, Father Smith, this is Cardinal O'Connor." And then I'd hear him say, "It's Cardinal O'Connor. Really. Yes, it's Cardinal O'Connor." We'd be roaring in the backseat, figuring some priest is saying to himself, "Who's this guy on the phone saying he's Cardinal O'Connor?"

NOT IMPRESSED, UNTIL ...

Brother Tyrone Davis is a member of the Congregation of Christian Brothers and a lawyer. Cardinal O'Connor appointed him to head the Office of Black Ministry for the New York Archdiocese on Nov. 1, 1995.

When I was in law school, people asked me if I would be going to work for the archdiocese. I never really wanted to. To be quite honest, I was not all that impressed with Cardinal O'Connor. I thought his style was very non-pastoral.

After law school, I got a position with the Brooklyn District Attorney's office, and after about three years there, somebody approached me about a position with the New York Archdiocese, in the Office of Black Ministry. I wound up accepting it. The job afforded me tremendous access to the Cardinal, not unlike the other staff directors. We had weekly staff meetings, which many of us occasionally moaned about but grew to appreciate. Quite unlike many of our counterparts in other archdioceses, we had access to the Cardinal Archbishop at least every week. I could count on the fact that once a week, I would have the ear of the Cardinal Archbishop to tell him about something I was doing or give him some inkling of an issue in the black community.

In those meetings, I often was sitting quite close to him. You get a good look at a person in those circumstances, and you get a good sense of what that person thinks is important.

There were some times when I got very frustrated with him, and probably he got frustrated with me. But I came to understand who he was, and I realized that he took some bold steps with me. They may not have been bold for everybody, but they were bold for him. For a Mass celebrating Black History Month in 1996— my first Mass in my position with the Office of Black Ministry—he allowed us to have a liturgical dancer. That was the first time, to my knowledge, that somebody was allowed to dance in St. Patrick's Cathedral. Everyone was extremely surprised that he said yes to that, and I think he was proud of himself after it happened, although he was pretty anxious during the week leading up to it. He called me on a Wednesday of that week on the pretense of calling about something else. He eventually asked me a few questions about the dancer. In the end, it was beautifully done. We didn't have her dance in the sanctuary; she danced up and down the aisles. And afterwards, in a style that was only Cardinal O'Connor's, he came down from his chair in the sanctuary, and he went over to the dancer—he ran down the stairs like he always did—and embraced her. It was really such a moment of warmth in that Cathedral. It was electric.

Here's the irony. When you consider how I looked upon him when I first came to the archdiocese, I would say that by the time I got a few years into this position, he became like a surrogate father to me. There are three people whom I consider as fathers: One was my own father, who died in 1999. Then there was the late Bishop Joseph Francis of the Newark Archdiocese, and the other person was Cardinal O'Connor.

AN ARC OF KNOWLEDGE

Kevin McCabe was chief of staff for Peter Vallone, Speaker of the New York City Council, in the late 1990s. A bluff, no-nonsense Queens guy from a blue-collar family, Mr. McCabe's work took him to the Cardinal's residence on several occasions. There, to his delight, he found somebody like himself as his host.

The Cardinal used to have us to breakfast at the residence, just the Speaker and me, His Eminence, and a few of his aides. It usually was general conversation, with each side bouncing ideas off the other.

The meeting I remember most was over what seemed like a small thing, but I got a real insight into a part of the Cardinal's personality that I don't think most people ever saw. The issue was about a landmarks bill in the Council, and it would have affected the Church as the owner of a lot of old buildings, most of them churches, around the city. I tried to explain the process to them, saying that there were different constituencies involved with this bill and laying out the pros and cons of the bill. I said that if we're going to get something done, we have to build some kind of consensus. Nuts and bolts government stuff.

One of the attendees on the Cardinal's side interupted and dismissed what I was saying. "That's not the answer I'm interested in," he said.

Immediately, the Cardinal jumps in, looks at this priest, and says, "Look, we have these guys over here for breakfast because we're interested in hearing what's going on out there. We have to be in touch with the people." And that was it. No more interuptions, and the conversation moved on to how we could get something accomplished.

The next time I met him, the topic was the persecution of Christians in China and elsewhere. Peter Vallone was looking to see what the city could do about it. The Cardinal was very appreciative, and I remember him talking about international issues, including the Middle East, with the same authority and knowledge that he had on little local issues. Here's a guy who was talking about zoning issues in one meeting and huge global issues in another. That's an amazing arc of knowledge. And through it all, you never forgot that you were in the room with somebody who knew exactly who he was— an Irish guy from a union family from Phildelphia, a guy who had peat under his nails.

IS THIS WHAT CHRIST WOULD DO?

During the last five years of his life, the Cardinal quietly met with a delegation of gay Catholics, many of whom were members of a gay Catholic group, Dignity, which had been banned from churches in the New York Archdiocese early on in the Cardinal's tenure. Jeff Stone is the spokesman for Dignity.

The leadership of Dignity asked to meet with Cardinal O'Connor not long after he took over as Archbishop of New York. From what I understand, the meeting was a disaster.

People expressed their hopes that there would be some change in the Church, some greater outreach to the gay and lesbian community. Apparently the Cardinal was quite hardline and just basically quoted official Church teaching at them.

So it was not positive, but the Cardinal did stay in touch with a fellow who was the head of Dignity at the time, Michael Olivieri. Michael died of AIDS somewhere in the middle-1990s, but before he died, he did continue to have a personal relationship with the Cardinal. But the Cardinal's relationship with Dignity and with the gay community was very tense. For Dignity, those tensions came to a height in 1987 when Dignity was asked to leave St. Francis Xavier Church, where it had been worshipping for at least 10 years. Dignity had been a recognized ministry within that parish. At the time, Dignity would have as many as 600 to 800 people at a liturgy. Some people in the archdiocese felt recognition of Dignity was pushing the envelope, that it seemed to signal an acceptance of gay relationships.

Though Cardinal O'Connor's name was not on any of the documents or communications, certainly it was very evident to all that this action to put Dignity out of Xavier would not have happened without his active support.

One segment of the group wanted to protest this vigorously. They would go to St. Patrick's once a month and would stand during the Cardinal's homily. That continued until the archdiocese got an injunction against it. Then, in 1989, there was the huge ACT-UP demonstration at the Cathedral, which was not supported by Dignity although some members did participate. Dignity argued against it prior to the event and criticized the actions afterwards.

Then, in 1995, the Cardinal made some remarks on Gay Pride Sunday of that year. It was quite a positive statement. He said, "Most people whose sexual orientation differs from the majority are good, decent people who try to lead responsible lives. They have their struggles as we all have our struggles. . . " And he went on, saying that violence would be inappropriate against anyone who would be marching in the parade today. He said, "I urge and pray that those who might be tempted to believe that in some way they are defending our faith through some form of violence ask themselves one question: Is this what Christ would do? The answer is clear."

That really came like a bolt out of the blue because the tone prior to that had been so different. So, a couple of people from Dignity said, "Why don't we write to him and suggest that we try to meet again. It's been years since we met officially, and this represents a new tone, so let's try and meet." About a month later, we wrote, and he responded favorably, and we had our first meeting with him on Nov. 30, 1995. We had six additional meetings, with the the last one on April 30, 1999.

He was extremely cordial to us personally, very polite and welcoming. Sometimes, when we were waiting for him in a sitting room, he would come out and bring us into his office himself, and we'd chat for a while. We shared with him our honest concerns, and he was direct with us as well. There were some moments certainly when the conversation was intense, but I think he always felt, as he told us during the second meeting, that the meetings were harmonious. We told him that we realized we were far apart on a number of issues of doctrine, and we weren't interested in going over that ground. He was happy with that. [Laughs]

We started off by talking about something we thought might be achievable, and that was reducing the tension around the Cathedral on Gay Pride Day every year. In the late '80s and early '90s it had kind of a fortress appearance. And then we talked broadly about the pastoral needs of gay, lesbian, bisexual, and transgendered people in the archdiocese—such issues ranging from youth suicides, the simple need for sensitivity among some pastors in handling confessions of gay and lesbian people, the fact that many people were involved in relationships and felt in need of counseling to make their relationships better, just as a heterosexual couple might need counseling.

The tone of the meetings was also very prayerful, and among the things we discussed was that we viewed ourselves as Catholics, and our intent was not to destroy the Church. The Cardinal saw his role as being a public teacher, and that included taking positions on public policy issues as a way of promoting Catholic teaching as he understood it. We appreciated that role. It is rooted in Catholic social justice tradition, and his statements in favor of workers' rights resonated with us. You have to take a position in the public arena—faith is not just a matter of private devotion, and while we disagreed with him on some issues, we agreed that communicating what you believe is part of what we're called to do.

There were three parishes in Manhattan that had gay ministries [unaffiliated with Dignity], and he encouraged us to meet with them. We formed an informal network which we all call the Roundtable of New York's Gay and Lesbian Catholic Ministries. We've done an Advent and Pentecost service every year.

In his heart, I think he understood that we were people trying to be Catholics. That was the starting point: We were talking to him as our pastor and our shepherd.

AN AIDS COMMISSION

Admiral Watkins

In 1987, I was made chairman of the presidential commission on AIDS. Cardinal O'Connor was on that commission. Two of the people on the commission had resigned, and President Reagan asked me to take it over. Cardinal O'Connor came to me and said, "Jim, I think I'm going to resign, too. I don't like where this might be going." I said, "Don't you dare. We aren't going to stress the use of condoms. We're going to get to the broad issues of health-care delivery, how we can mitigate this problem, where we should put our resources, how should we deal with home health care. We're not going to get into areas that are counter to your beliefs. I'm on your side on this." So he stayed on the commission. I think Cardinal O'Connor was very pleased with our final report. The word "condom" was used once in about 250 pages, and never in the context of a quick fix for the disease.

Only God has ultimate power over life. That power cannot be arrogated by any human being, a doctor, a judge, a legislator, a patient, a proxy—any human being.
—*Cardinal O'Connor's column,*
Catholic New York

CARDINAL O'CONNOR was one of the world's most passionate voices on behalf of all human life. He opposed capital punishment, decried the slippery slope some dared call "mercy killing," and celebrated the holiness of the disabled. Most of all, he preached against abortion. He founded an order of nuns, the Sisters of Life, who pray endlessly for an end to abortion. He asked Catholic Charities to work with women in crisis pregnancies. And he criticized public policies that promoted abortion. His words prompted headlines, but his actions behind the scenes went unnoticed.

A ROSE ON HIS LAPEL

Sandi Merle is a Jewish grandmother who lives a few blocks away from St. Patrick's Cathedral. Her friendship with the Cardinal grew out of a conversation she overheard between the Cardinal and a friend. Her life was never quite the same.

We first met shortly after he came to New York, at a reception given by the New York Board of Rabbis. I am on the media commission for the Board. That first meeting, it was like God had said, "These people should meet and know each other's hearts."

I was standing in a line, I remember it very well, to greet him. Ahead of me was a dear girlfriend of mine, and she noticed that the Cardinal was wearing a rose on his coat. And she said, "Oh, is that the rose of Sharon?" [A reference to a prophetic line in Song of Songs.] And he said, "No, dear lady. That is the rose that grows in my heart for all of the roses not allowed to grow." That line put me away, and it it still does. [Pauses] I feel like a crybaby. By the time I got to the front of the line, I was distraught. He said to me, "Are you all right?" He had no idea that I heard what he said, or why I was crying, and he inquired about my health. I said, "No, no, no. I'm fine. It's just that you should never hear what you should never hear. I guess I had no business overhearing your conversation with my friend. But it affected me very much." We talked for a short while, and he asked me to stay later, but I couldn't. I was really distraught. I couldn't wait to get home and really have a good cry, realizing what abortion was doing to him and the pain it was causing this man.

When I got home I decided to write to him, and it took me a few days to get up the courage to do that. I am a Jewish female in the arts, and I always kept my convictions quite private. But that's when the turn in my life began. And I realized that whatever I believed, if it was for the betterment of mankind, I had to shout it.

Some time later, he wrote back to me. I have the letter right here. He wrote:

"Dear Sandi:

"It would be impossible for me to count the number of letters of every description that I have received since becoming Archbishop of New York. Your letter of December 25"—that's a coincidence, isn't it?—"however, is equal to any I have ever received from anyone from any religion or station in life in terms of the sheer joy it had given me. There is no way in which I can adequately express my gratitude. Please assure your friends that I am deeply appreciative of their confidence in me, and for their prayers on my behalf."

And then there was this line:

"I am particularly grateful that you continue to carry the red rose in your heart."

That's when I realized I had to do what I had to do. Friendship just bloomed from there. We carried on a correspondence of hundreds of letters, and we would meet at

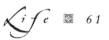

functions, mainly Jewish functions where he was being honored. He would invite me to an occasional gathering in his home, too. I eventually founded an organization called STOP, and that stands for Standing Together to Oppose Partial Birth Abortion. STOP was made up of Jewish females in the arts because that was the toughest group to get. I thought, well, anybody can do what's easy. I will do the impossible, or at least try. We became a mighty little force. We went to Washington and lobbied the House and Senate.

THE SISTERS OF LIFE

In March of 1991, Agnes Donovan was an assistant professor at Columbia University and Teachers College. She had a Ph.D. in child development and family studies, had taught at William & Mary College, and had been a school pyschologist in Ithaca, N.Y. She was at a turning point in her life, and, in search of answers, she went on a four-day retreat with 10 other women who were thinking about entering religious life. Cardinal O'Connor was the retreat's host, and was making plans to found a new religious community, the Sisters of Life. The order began in June, 1991, with eight sisters. There are now 37 and Agnes Mary Donovan is their mother superior.

A profound memory I have of Cardinal O'Connor was the way he spoke so wonderfully about religious life and the sacredness of human life during that retreat. I remember sitting at the table one night—he would join us for dinner, hold three or four conferences a day, celebrate Mass—and I was saying to myself, "My goodness, you're sitting opposite a present-day apostle." I didn't know Cardinals, that wasn't part of my life. But I realized that he was a man of palpable faith. You could sense that, experience that, in his presence.

I left the retreat, not sure what to do. Knowing myself, I had thought, "I'll really know after this weekend whether this is for me or not." I was quite convinced that I would enter religious life, but I really didn't know where. And I remember I said to the Cardinal, "You know, I really beg you to pray for me." And he said, "I will. I will." And I left, and about two weeks later I just awoke one day and I knew I would enter that community, the Sisters of Life. And I really take it as a grace. I don't think I could explain it in any other way.

He was very frank. He often said he was doing what he believed the Holy Spirit had asked him, and if it was of the Holy Spirit, then it would turn out all right. I had great trust in him. When he founded the order, I said, "He will lead us in a trustworthy way toward authentic religious life."

With the Sisters of Life, he was very fatherly. That was his role for us; there was little formality. He was very interested in the personal struggles of sisters, and he invited them to visit him if he felt they needed some personal guidance or direction. He would meet with the community once every two weeks or so, and would host two retreats a year, which all the Sisters attended.

Once, when the community was still quite young, we were going to buy a car so we could get around. We said, "Let's get a 15-seater van and we can go together wherever we had to go." There were about 12 or 14 of us at the time.

He would not hear of it. He said we weren't going to get a van because, he said, "What if you drive off a bridge someday, I'll lose the whole community." [Laughs] That was the end of the van. He really was quite protective of us.

A PRESIDENTIAL DIS-INVITATION

Jennifer Lynch

I worked on the Al Smith [fundraising] dinner, which was run out of the archdiocese's development office. I remember the 1996 dinner, when President Clinton and [his then-opponent] Bob Dole were disinvited. They both had accepted, but then Clinton vetoed the ban on partial birth abortions that had passed Congress. The Cardinal was very outspoken that he would not have Clinton at the dinner. He didn't shy away from that. He said he wouldn't want the President to come and be uncomfortable at the dinner, which he would have been.

So we went through a number of options. The Al Smith dinner was a big deal in a presidential election year. The candidates always came. Some of the lay people in the office felt it was important to have both candidates come. They asked, "How can you disinvite a President?" The Cardinal was adamant that we couldn't have President Clinton, and so we couldn't have Senator Dole because that would be like an endorsement. And that's the way it went.

JEWISH, ATHEIST, PRO-LIFE

Growing up in Boston in the late 1930s and early 1940s, Nat Hentoff came to regard the Catholic Church as "ever-present, mysterious, and my enemy." He was a Jew in a city he regarded as the most anti-Semitic urban area in America.

Long after he left Boston, Mr. Hentoff became, in his own phrase, a Jewish-atheist-pro-life-civil-libertarian. "When I first met John O'Connor, I described myself that way, and he asked me to repeat it," Mr. Hentoff said. "He looked at me like he had just discovered a new sect." It was their shared opposition to abortion that brought the Cardinal and the Jewish-atheist together. Mr. Hentoff wrote a profile of the newly arrived Archbishop for The New Yorker, *which was expanded to a full biography, entitled* John Cardinal O'Connor: At the Storm Center of a Changing American Catholic Church. *(Charles Scribners & Sons, 1987)*

The question of how he was portrayed in the media goes back to the question of bias in the press. Anti-Catholicism is the last refuge of people who don't think they're biased. However subliminally, most journalists in New York City would not hold in high regard somebody who was an icon of pro-life activity. It reminds me of how the *Washington Post* used to cover the pro-life and pro-choice rallies held to commemorate the anniversary of *Roe v. Wade*. The coverage leading up to the pro-choice rallies would include lists of speakers, maps of the protest area, etc. The pro-life rallies got nothing until after the fact. An editor finally said, "Look, what's going on here?" And somebody said, "Well, we don't know anybody who's pro-life." It's sort of the same thing with O'Connor. Except for some Catholic reporters, the journalists didn't know anybody like Cardinal O'Connor, who was engaging and complicated and pro-life. They decided he was too Catholic. As far as what the Cardinal said about social justice, well, those issues don't matter to some people.

A BULLET-PROOF VEST

Joe Zwilling

He was a lightning rod, and he didn't mind it. Pretty late in his life, as it turned out, he said to me, "I've been the subject of a lot of criticism, but there are very few people in this town who don't know where the Catholic Church stands on things. Maybe they don't have all the nuance, but they know the Church is against abortion. They know the Church teaches about the rights and dignity of working people." So he had no complaints, but I don't think he liked being attacked personally.

I remember walking with him when he was marching from St. Agnes Church in midtown Manhattan to an abortion clinic to pray the Rosary. At the time, he had been the subject of death threats, and the police had a bulletproof vest on him. During the Mass at St. Agnes, protestors had been banging drums and making noises to drown out the sounds of the Mass. As we walked towards the abortion clinic, demonstrators were lined up on both sides of the street. They were shouting the most vile things. You could feel the hatred. I don't think he enjoyed that, but he was willing to accept it for doing what he thought the Church was calling him to do.

CUOMO AND THE CARDINAL

In the media and in the public's perception, John Cardinal O'Connor and former Governor Mario Cuomo of New York were antagonists—famously so. In 1984, when Mr. Cuomo was emerging as a star of national politics and Geraldine Ferraro was making history as the first woman on a national ticket, the Cardinal spoke out against Catholic politicians who supported abortion rights, as Mr. Cuomo and Ms. Ferraro did. Mr. Cuomo replied with an address at Notre Dame University that solidified the image of the Cardinal and the Governor as enemies. But the relationship between these two Catholic intellectuals was a good deal more complex. In December, 1999, with the Cardinal gravely ill, Mario Cuomo wrote a tribute to him on the Op-Ed Page of The New York Times. *The piece set the tone for the tributes that, five months later, appeared in the Cardinal's obituaries. Here he recounts his view of their problems over the abortion issue.*

When the Cardinal came to New York—this most difficult of archdioceses because of the tremendous force of the media here—he made a couple of statements expressing his abhorrence for abortion and for politicians who appeared in any way to be condoning it in his eyes. Geraldine Ferraro was one on them. Then he was asked on a radio show whether Mario Cuomo should be excommunicated. Just by coincidence, Matilda [Cuomo's wife] and I and our youngest son, Christopher, were listening. The word went though me like a dagger. I was shocked by the question. And he answered it with some equivocation, which made it worse.

Now, he never did say that I should be excommunicated, and our relationship became entirely different as the years went on, but at that moment, it was a time of terror for me. I didn't sleep that night, and the next morning, I said to Matilda over coffee that the problem here is that nobody has ever addressed this issue fully as a politician. We run away from it, duck it, because it is so difficult to handle. I decided I needed to explain to myself, and then to everybody else, what exactly the issue is—what it is for me as a Catholic, what it is for me as a public official, and what is the difference between those two capacities. And I did that. I started that day and wrote for about five weeks, as I recall. I talked with [aides] Peter Quinn and Bill Hanlon, two of the smartest people I've ever met and two of the best writers I ever met. Over the weeks, we discussed the issue from all angles, and finally had a piece that I thought would describe as accurately as I could how I felt on this issue.

By coincidence, I had been invited to address a religion class at Notre Dame University in September. I called the priest who invited me, and I said, "I think I'd better cancel this, because if I come there to speak, there's sure to be press and you'll be embarrassed because of this controversial subject." The priest said he'd talk to [Notre Dame President] Father Theodore Hesburgh, who said, "No, that's not right. Let him come here and say what he wants to say. If we don't like it, we'll be free to say so." So I said, "Gee, if that's what you want, we'll do it."

And we did. Then came the Notre Dame speech, and that was the beginning, but by no means the end, of my relationship with Cardinal O'Connor. Thereafter, I got to know the Cardinal in a lot of different ways.

My position on abortion as stated in that paper was clear: I am a Roman Catholic. If I wish to remain a Roman Catholic, which I devoutly do, then I accept the Church teaching. This does not mean that I understand it perfectly, or that I could arrive at exactly the same conclusion through the use of my intellect, but if the Church teaches formally that life begins at conception, I am required to accept that. And I do. You have to live by the law. But that's not the question for a governor. A governor is not in charge of the Supreme Court, and cannot write an amendment to the federal Constitution, and so cannot change the law anyway. Therefore, on the main question of abortion, it's really an opinion that you're giving, and my opinion is that in order for us as Catholics to persuade the whole society that abortion is evil because life begins at conception, before we can expect the whole society to accept that Catholic teaching, we would as Catholics have to live by it ourselves.

A CHANGE OF HEART

Mario Cuomo was not the only Catholic politician drawn into the abortion controversy. In the mid-1980s, John Dearie was an assemblyman from the Bronx who was thought to have a bright future in New York politics. Like nearly all of his Democratic colleagues, he voted in favor of state Medicaid funding for abortions. As a result, in 1986 the archdiocese announced that he no longer was welcome to speak at Church functions. The episode made national headlines. Mr. Dearie retired from politics in 1992, and now practices law in New York.

I was surprised by the action taken against me. When we met to discuss what had happened, he was very firm, very stern. He never asked me to do anything. He was firm and clear. He supported the pro-life position both theologically and morally, and there was no equivocation. He never at any point threatened me; he simply asked me to pray and think about my position. He said to me, "You're the kind of person we need supporting our position."

I did pray and I did think a lot. I began thinking about going with my wife, Kitty, and seeing those sonograms of our son in the womb. It had a profound impact, the notion of life and what it meant. And I did change my position. There was some feeling that, "Oh, it was just a matter of time before O'Connor's politics got to him." But it was the Cardinal's *thoughts* that got to me.

After I changed my position, the Cardinal had my wife

and me to dinner at his residence. He had a remarkable way of showing his thanks. As stern as he was in the beginning, there was a great feeling of love about him. And he was concerned about what my decision would mean to me in both a political and a personal sense.

ATHLETES FOR LIFE

Wellington Mara is a co-owner of the New York Giants and a member of the Board of Trustees of St. Patrick's Cathedral. The Maras are a devout Irish-Catholic family, known for the philanthropic work and their involvement in pro-life activities.

The Cardinal was very involved with Life Athletes, a pro-life group started by Chris Godfrey, an offensive guard on our Super Bowl team, a few years ago. Phil Simms was an honoree at one of our dinners, and [former tight end] Mark Bavaro was very active, too, and they made a few appearances with the Cardinal. We staged a number of fundraisers and dinners, and the Cardinal without fail would show up to support them. We had several breakfast meetings at Yonkers Raceway because the owner, Tim Rooney, is a member of the Life Athletes board; the Cardinal used to make every one of them—at eight o'clock in the morning, all the way up in Yonkers.

A lot of this work wasn't known to the public. That's because, I think, the Cardinal used up so much ink with other things that the behind-the-scenes work never became known. While he didn't go looking for confrontations, he didn't avoid any either. [Laughs] You always knew where he stood on everything.

"I DIDN'T WANT TO LIVE"

Margarita came to New York from Latin America after learning she was pregnant. Margarita is not her real name—she asked that she remain anonymous, and that the circumstances of her pregnancy remain private. Somehow, she found herself in St. Patrick's Cathedral as she contemplated suicide.

At the age of 29, I was at the peak of my professional career. Then, I got pregnant in the most unthinkable way that a woman can get pregnant. I thought I had lost my mind. I thought, "How can a baby come to life in these circumstances?" It's not the first time that this has happened; it has happened so many times in history, and it is happening right now. It's one thing when you hear about it, but when it happens to you, it's not comprehensible.

I thought the best thing for me was to come to New York because I had a brother who was living here. I arrived the day the Pope was visiting here, October 7th, 1995. The morning I arrived, the Pope was in Central Park. I left my bags at my brother's apartment and walked through the streets, and I found myself outside St. Patrick's Cathedral. There were barricades around, because the Pope was coming later. But I just went in and I sat there for a long time, and I left. Two days later, I went there again, and I fainted in front of St. Joseph's altar. Somebody saw me and picked me up. I spoke with a priest who asked me what happened. I couldn't stop crying. I told him my story, and he said, "OK, give me your name and telephone number, because I think somebody should know about this." So next morning I get a phone call that I should go to the back of St. Patrick's the next day after Mass. I went—but I couldn't care less about why I was going, because I didn't want to live.

The Cardinal was there, and after the 7:30 Mass, he met me in the back of the church. I had never heard his name before. I didn't know who he was, and I didn't care. To me, he was just a priest from the church. He asked, "What is your name?" I couldn't stop crying, and he said, "I guess it's going to be difficult," and I started laughing. And then he asked me how he could help me. He didn't ask me what had happened—he asked me how he could help. So I told him the story, and he said, "Don't worry. What is it that you need?" I didn't know what I needed—I wanted to die. So he said, "The first thing you need is a doctor." And with that, he opened the door for me to come back to life. He talked to people who led me to the right places to get the help I needed—physically, emotionally, mentally, spiritually. The things he did were little miracles, and pretty soon, incredibly, I was back on my feet again and I wanted to live. He was like a father to me, no, even more—I could see God through him.

Then, my son was born. I named him Patrick Joseph, and he said to me, "Joseph is my middle name, too." I wanted my son to be baptized right away, and I went to see the priest I met on the day I fainted in the Cathedral. He said, "I would like to do the baptism, but I know the Cardinal wants to do that, so I'll step aside." And the Cardinal picked the day and the time—the date he picked was the anniversary of the founding of the Sisters of Life—and he baptized Patrick that morning.

Even after Patrick was born, the Cardinal kept in touch with me and helped me. One day, there was an event in the seminary, and there were hundreds of people present. I was there with Patrick, who was still a baby, and he was crying and tired. I went outside and two minutes later, the car pulls up with the Cardinal inside, and the doors open and he sees me and says, "Oh, there you are." And he talked to me for a while. It was like that all the time—the little things, the little miracles. Another time I saw him walking into a church for a big event, and he saw me and came over to me and gave me a big hug. How was he thinking about me when he was doing something else? Another time, I saw him at a public ceremony on a Sunday morning, and I gave him a note which he put into his pocket. Then, later on, we were having lunch at my house and the phone rings. My brother answered it and then handed me the phone and said, "It's Cardinal O'Connor."

Those were the kinds of things he did. I consider him to be the instrument that God used to bring me back to life, and to allow me to have my son alive. After I met him, everything began to fall into place. He helped me get a new job. And he showed me how to go from hating a situation to loving someone so much. I brought Patrick to see him sometimes, and the Cardinal would have candy there, and my son wanted some. And the Cardinal would say, "Ask Mommy if I can give it to you."

What always impressed me was how very ordinary things were done in such extraordinary ways, how a very ordinary man—which is how he considered himself—was so extraordinary. You know how God takes care of us individually? Cardinal O'Connor did the same thing for me, and he did it for many other people. What he did for me he would have done for anybody.

THE TOUGHEST QUESTION

William Flynn is chairman of Mutual of America, an insurance and financial services company, and a past president of the Knights of Malta, a charitable Catholic organization. The two men met early in the Cardinal's New York years.

He was very easy, very friendly, which was quite a surprise to me, frankly. When somebody is a Cardinal Archbishop, and also an Admiral who has seen combat, you conjure up a certain kind of person—steely, strong, willful—it kind of goes with the image. What I found, however, was once you sat down and had a cup of tea with him, he was just a simple Catholic priest.

The toughest questions he was ever asked, he told me, came from those single women who were pregnant and were faced with the decision of life or no life. "What will I do? How will I survive?" He bemoaned the fact that he had no place for them. So he went to the Knights of Malta and asked

them to make this their top priority, looking after some of these women. And so we did. He took on these difficult jobs, and did what he could with limited resources. I admired that about the man.

A RITE OF PENTECOST

Cardinal O'Connor's passion for life included a range of issues beyond abortion. He opposed assisted suicide and capital punishment, and he preached that all human life is precious. He practiced his preaching early in his priesthood, when he ministered to disabled children. Later, as Archbishop of New York, he commemorated Pentecost Sunday, when the Holy Spirit descended upon the Apostles, with a special Confirmation Mass for the developmentally and physically disabled. Joe Zwilling recalls those moving ceremonies.

Everywhere he went he established a program for the disabled, particularly for the mentally retarded. The confirmation ceremony for the handicapped in the Cathedral was one of the most beautiful and moving days of the year—to watch the love he had for them, to hear the words of encouragement he had for their parents. It goes back to his not wanting to lose his sense of priesthood. This was not the kind of thing you'd expect a Navy chaplain to do, but he did it. And that love he expressed, it was so genuine. You could see it.

HE HELD HER. HE HUGGED HER.

Eileen Dennehy, who has Down syndrome, received the sacra-ment of Confirmation on Pentecost Sunday, 1998. Her mother, Mary Dennehy, witnessed the ceremony.

Eileen made her Confirmation along with another boy from St. Columba parish [in Chester, N.Y.] who was in a wheelchair. There were about 35 other people with special needs who were going to be confirmed. The Cardinal physically touched every one of the young people and said something positive to each one. There were many people in the congregation that day who never had to deal with a special needs person, so it was a great message they were receiving.

He spent a lot of time with the young people, and I know all the parents and family members were touched by his words and thoughts. When the Mass was over, he stood on the altar and took pictures with each of the families. Each picture must have taken about five minutes, and there were about 35 families, so it took a lot of time. But he made sure every family had a picture with the Cardinal. We have ours hanging in the family room.

It wasn't the first time I met him. He came to our parish just after he was installed as Archbishop, in 1984 or 1985. He was standing outside the church before Mass, greeting parishioners. Eileen was about a year old at the time, and I was holding her in my arms. He immediately reached out for her, held her, hugged her, and blessed her. Later on during his remarks to the congregation, he mentioned that he had met me and my daughter. He really had a soft spot in his heart for handicapped children.

We're very fortunate that Eileen is high-functioning and doing well. Other families we've gotten to know have children who are more severely handicapped. A lot of work and time goes into raising these children. Nobody is looking for sympathy, but the outside world doesn't realize what it takes. The Cardinal made these families feel very good.

PROTECTING ABANDONED INFANTS

Sandi Merle

I told the Cardinal I just couldn't stand reading stories in the papers about dead babies being found in garbage cans. I said there had to be a way to get those mothers to stop killing their children. I told him there should be a law where these mothers, most of whom are young and frightened, know that there's something else that they can do. There was a black-tie affair at the Waldorf sponsored by the Museum of Jewish Heritage around 1998. Robert Morgenthau, the Manhattan district attorney, was in attendance, as was the Cardinal, and halfway through the evening the Cardinal turned to me and asked if I knew Bob Morgenthau. I said I didn't. He said, "Well, you will before the night is over." He introduced me to Morgenthau later, and he told him, "You are going to hear something from this young lady, Bob. Listen to her." And that was it. I knew, of course, why that was done. One thing led to another, and last year [2000], a bill was passed in the State Assembly called the Abandoned Infant Survival Law. Rosie O'Donnell is now doing promotions for it. It allows women to leave their newborn infants in hospitals and other facilities without fear of prosecution. They do it anonymously, no questions asked.

We did a press conference in spring, 2001, to talk about the new law, and I knew that we were not there alone. This was something the Cardinal knew I could pull off if he introduced me to the right person. Do you know what it felt like the first time I heard that a baby in Brooklyn, who was still in utero at the time, had a mother who said, "I want to give this baby up. I don't want to kill it." I really felt that I fulfilled a paragraph of the Talmud, which says, and I quote, "He who saves a life, saves the world entire."

All of this, all of this, is because of the rose on his coat.

Reconciliation

We disgrace our divine Lord, we disgrace
Catholicism, whenever we are guilty of
anti-Semitism.
—Cardinal O'Connor's Sunday homily,
June 13, 1999

CARDINAL O'CONNOR often said his formative
experience as an adult was his visit to Dachau,
where he held the ashes of its victims in his
hands. As a Cardinal-Archbishop in the city
with more Jews than any other in the world,
John O'Connor became a symbol of reconciliation and healing between Catholics and Jews.

A BRIDGE OF PEACE

Rabbi Leon Klenicki is a native of Argentina who headed the Department of Interfaith Affairs of the Anti-Defamation League. Rabbi Klenicki began his relationship with Cardinal O'Connor under less than ideal circumstances, when he wrote a letter to him protesting comments the Cardinal had made equating abortions to the Holocaust. Out of this initial misunderstanding, a warm friendship and an enduring partnership grew, based on their commitment to fostering relations and understanding between the Catholic and Jewish communities. They eventually published a booklet together entitled, A Challenge Long Delayed, *about the establishment of diplomatic relations between the Holy See and Israel, an historic undertaking to which both men contributed. Mr. Klenicki also accompanied Cardinal O'Connor to Argentina, where he watched the Cardinal deliver a thundering homily decrying bigotry.*

I met him in the very beginning, when he first came to New York as the new Archbishop. He gave a speech in which he said that abortion was "the Auschwitz of American life." I heard this, and I wrote to him immediately, and said that I thought it was very improper to use words like "Auschwitz" to describe abortion. In the United States, I said, a woman can have the child, put the child up for adoption, or have an abortion—

there are several possibilities. In Europe, for a Jew, we had no possibilities. As a Jew, you were destined for death.

He was very touched by that, I think, and he wrote an essay in the newsletter of the Anti-Defamation League explaining what he meant by that. It was very important to him.

Not long after that he decided to go to Israel. He went to Yad Vashem, the Holocaust Memorial in Jerusalem, and he wrote "A Note from Yad Vashem," which was also published. He stressed the horror of the Holocaust and said that it is a Jewish tragedy and that we have to be careful how we use language in relation to the Holocaust.

We had an ongoing and very close relationship after that. We would visit each other and talk over the problems of our communities. Sometimes, when there were confrontations between the Catholic and Jewish communities, I would go to him, because I knew he would understand. This was an ongoing thing. He talked to Jewish audiences, and encouraged me to teach in a Catholic seminary. He was also very much interested in programs about education and the presentation of the New Testament and Judaism.

On an international level, he was also very active in communicating with the Holy See and getting diplomatic recognition for Israel. O'Connor would always say later on that the help he provided in all this was exaggerated, and that whatever he did by way of visits to Israel and Rome, and in his writings and homilies, was minuscule next to the events themselves. In fact, I think he played a very important role. But he was always very generous with extending credit to others. He told me that I was "an abiding friend of the Catholic-Jewish encounter."

Reconciliation ◉ 83

The Cardinal was also a personal friend during moments of great agony. I lost a daughter in a car accident, and it took me a long time to recover. Whenever we would meet after that, we would talk about it. He would say a word or touch my arm. When he talked to me, it was as a friend. He was not the Cardinal, he was a pastor listening to someone in pain. He would also remember my daughter, Myriam, every February at Mass at St. Patrick's Cathedral. He never forgot to mention her and say a prayer for her. I once even got a call from a Catholic friend of mine in Rome. He had been at a meeting with O'Connor, and at this meeting he had mentioned Myriam. In Rome! [Pauses] That was precious.

PARADING FOR ISRAEL

A political activist and former president of the Jewish Community Relations Council, Martin Begun was a witness to Cardinal O'Connor's fierce dedication to the State of Israel. In 1998, Mr. Begun brokered an historic and symbolically important agreement for the Cardinal to make an appearance at that year's Salute to Israel Day Parade.

I remember when I went to see Cardinal O'Connor in his First Avenue office. It was a meeting that came at a pretty rough time for me personally. My mother had passed away a week or two before. I guess the Cardinal knew that—he had already sent me a note, before we met, expressing his condolences—and when I came, he took both my hands and told me how sorry he was.

So we sat there in his office, with Father Pat Loughlin, who was the liaison to community-based Jewish groups, around a coffee table. The Cardinal was immediately very disarming, joking around. Father Loughlin, it turned out, had forgotten his collar. So, of course, the Cardinal, being a former chaplain in the Navy, pretends to scold him for being out of uniform. He was joking, of course, but that got us all to laugh. It lightened things up. The Cardinal talked about New York, what he wanted to do here, and those sorts of things. He also told me, very generously, that I should always call him if he could ever help us out with anything.

Before this meeting, I had discussed the idea with my colleagues of inviting the Cardinal to the Israeli Parade. It was an unusual idea—it would have been the first time a Cardinal had attended the event. Now, the meeting was going so well, that I decided to do it. So as the meeting was drawing to an end, I said, with some trepidation, "I would very much like to extend an invitation to Your Eminence. . . " Before I even finished he said, "I would love to." He turned to Father Loughlin and told him to make sure that his schedule would be free. His enthusiasm at that point was such that I decided to go for broke—I asked him if he would consider getting some Catholic students in marching bands to participate in the parade. He not only agreed, but said that he would help in any other way he could. I think Father Loughlin was the only one who might not have been delighted because his workload was doubling by the minute. But I was thrilled.

Reconciliation ❖ 85

It turned out to be a very nasty day, and we were prepared to inform the Cardinal's office that we understood if he wasn't up to it. But sure enough, when the parade kicked off, the Cardinal arrived, and went to take his place in the reviewing stand. He stayed for a long time, shook hands with the marchers, spoke to everyone. It was really tremendous.

A QUESTION OF FLAGS

Monsignor Finn

When he was in the military, and services were conducted on a military base, a Church flag with a cross was raised, representing Christianity. There was some question about whether there should be a flag representing the Jewish faith. He readily agreed, and put in a request. It went through the chain of command, and nothing happened. It went nowhere. He finally said, "Well, let's go to the top," and he called the Secretary of the Navy, or maybe even the Defense Secretary, and he got the flag. When he put his mind to something, it got done.

EXTRAORDINARY SENSITIVITY

◈

Rabbi Michael Miller, the longtime head of the Jewish Community Relations Council and a member of the Orthodox Caucus, partnered with Cardinal O'Connor on numerous high-profile interfaith endeavors. "He was a pastor to all New Yorkers," the rabbi said. "He was our Cardinal. Jewish New Yorkers felt that close to him."

My initial encounter with him was through an interfaith coalition concerned about cults. The archdiocese had been one of the founding members of this coalition, as they had a particular interest in combating satanism. The Cardinal was the keynote speaker at a meeting, and that was when I introduced myself to him. I learned to greatly appreciate his identification with the Jewish community and with Israel.

In November, 1988, we held a 50th anniversary event for the commemoration of Kristallnacht, when Nazis attacked Jewish shops in prewar Germany, and we invited the Cardinal to be our keynote speaker. I don't know how many communities would invite their Cardinal or Bishop to be their keynote speaker for an event commemorating the Holocaust. But Cardinal O'Connor was a cherished friend by then.

The commemoration was held at Congregation Kehilath Jeshuren, on 85th Street between Park and Lexington, an Orthodox synagogue. So the Prince of the Church in New York was addressing a subject matter regarding the Holocaust in an Orthodox synagogue in Manhattan. There were so many aspects to this event and his participation in it that were unique. Foremost was his speech. I recall quite vividly how he referred to himself as a "spiritual Semite." It was remarkable. I wouldn't presume to try to explain why he felt that connection to the Jewish community, but he clearly felt a kinship.

Also, if I remember correctly, the Cardinal was dressed in his black tunic and his red belt and his hat, and, of course, a big gold cross. He tucked the cross into his tunic. It was a measure of his sensitivity. I think that was a display of the measure of the man. He always seemed to know what to do around us. He just possessed extraordinary sensitivity.

To me, he was a quintessential fatherly figure. He was someone with whom I felt very comfortable talking through issues and personal concerns, as if he were my rabbi. I always felt very much at ease in his presence. That was a gift he had.

IN THE POPE'S IMAGE

Rabbi Joseph Erenkranz is director of the Center for Christian-Jewish Understanding at Sacred Heart University, Fairfield, Conn. He was one of several eulogists at a special memorial service sponsored by New York's Jewish community and conducted in St. Patrick's Cathedral the day before the Cardinal's funeral.

Cardinal O'Connor was extremely sensitive to the feelings of the Jewish people. I went to him once with the idea of holding a memorial in St. Patrick's for the great baseball announcer Mel Allen, who was Jewish. He grabbed onto the idea, because he understood how this would bring together members of the Jewish and Catholic communities. The event drew a thousand people. He had an uncanny ability to bring people together. There was nobody in the world, in fact, who understood better the need to bring together the Catholic and Jewish communities. If I might say so, he was in the image of Pope John Paul II. We [the Center for Christian-Jewish Understanding] had a number of award ceremonies, and he lent us the use of his personal residence for cocktail parties and such. He always took things one step further than he had to.

I remember a number of instances when he spoke about the sense of spirituality that guided all of us. Even though I expect every rabbi, every Cardinal, to be guided by spirituality, too many of us are too pragmatic. He overlooked the pragmatic, and he backed up his contentions with facts.

Even when he didn't agree, he was able to communicate his warmth. He focused on you, and what your needs were. You were a person to him.

AN HISTORIC APOLOGY

Howard Rubenstein is the head of Rubenstein Associates, a powerhouse public relations firm whose list of clients ranges from the New York Yankees to media mogul Rupert Murdoch to Sarah Ferguson. His office, on the 30th floor of a building in midtown Manhattan, is decorated with caps, hats, and helmets representing an astonishing array of causes, crusades, and clients. He and Cardinal O'Connor worked together on several projects promoting greater Catholic-Jewish understanding. "If he had asked me, I would have done even more for him," he said. "That's the kind of person he was."

I had been doing some publicity work for the Inner City Scholarship Fund, and we were doing really well. And then he asked me to join the Fund's board—there weren't many Jewish people on it, maybe one other. I got really friendly with him, and I joined him at some of the schools he visited. I became very, very enthusiastic about what he was doing, and what I was doing. I encouraged clients to give money to the fund, and many did.

Parallel to this, we were about to do the dedication of our new building at the Holocaust Museum here in New York. I suggested to Manhattan District Attorney Bob Morgenthau, another founder of the museum, that we invite the Cardinal to speak. Some of the Orthodox Jewish people fought it. They said, "He's Catholic; there were some problems with Catholics during World War II, the Holocaust period." They were pretty vocal, but it had nothing to do with the Cardinal personally. Bob Morgenthau and I overruled everybody. We just said, "It's done." And they said, "Well, maybe he shouldn't say a prayer." And we said, "He'll say whatever he wants to say." Then I spoke to him, and I suggested that this is an opportunity to say whatever he cared to say, in any format that he wished.

He came to that dedication, and he delivered the first speech I ever heard issuing an apology to the Jewish community for what happened during the Holocaust. The handful of people who resisted his participation thanked him and thanked me and thanked Bob Morgenthau for standing up for what we thought was right. I loved the man from that moment on. I'd always liked him, but I loved him for what he did that day.

After that, I became chairman of the nominating committee of the Inner City Scholarship Fund. So they have a Jewish person as chairman. Boy, I found that amusing in a way, and very interesting. Now I take orders from the Cardinal. [Laughs] I just thought it was very gracious of him and very nice of him to do that.

Once, I was talking to him about the Holocaust Museum, and the head of the Catholic school system, Catherine Hickey, was with him. I said to him, "We're hopeful that the Catholic schoolchildren will come to that museum." And he directed Dr. Hickey to see to it that the Catholic school classes visited—we've had something like 25,000 Catholic schoolchildren come. That was another very significant move in terms of understanding one another, in terms of understanding what the Holocaust did to us, and in terms of making sure that it never happens again to any other group.

Reconciliation ▨ 91

HE WAS OURS

Sandi Merle

He was a Catholic who never lost touch with his Jewish roots. He would yell at us, and say, "Be proud of who you are. Be proud of the gifts that you have given the country and the world."

I started attending Sunday Mass at St. Patrick's Cathedral as often as possible because of the Cardinal's homily, naturally not for the Mass. I am a traditional Jew, always have been and will remain so. But the homilies were hours that I could not deny myself. As a matter of fact, I learned more about Judaism than I had known before. There are many things not in the Jewish canon which the Cardinal was able to talk about— Macabees, for example. And it was just so beautiful to hear it from him, because it was done with compassion and love. He was the good priest, the good shepherd, and he wasn't only yours. He was mine. He was ours.

One of the last things we worked together on was a partnership between the Assaf Harofeh Medical Center in Israel and Our Lady of Mercy/St. Agnes Medical Center in New York. It's the first time in history that a Jewish hospital and a Catholic hospital have formed a partnership. Now this started as a dream of mine for the Jubilee Year [2000]. I thought, "My goodness, there are going to be so many people traveling to Israel for the jubilee, and Assaf is right near Ben-Gurion Airport between Tel Aviv and Jerusalem. How about making it so that people on pilgrimages know there is a place prepared for them?"

I got in touch with the Cardinal, who thought it was a fabulous idea. We worked and we worked, and suddenly our leader is ill. And I went to him one day, and I said, "I know you want this. Tell me that you want me to pull it through." He said, "Yes. We must go where we are needed." And that's all I needed to drive me forward. The formal affiliation was made two weeks after he died, on May 14, 2000. Mary Ward planted a beautiful evergreen tree in Israel for her brother. We compare the significance of planting trees in Judaism to the Torah, about which we say, "It is a tree of life for all who choose to grasp it." And as Mary Ward said that day, "My brother shall grow as a tree of life for all who have chosen to grasp what he taught."

HE SOUNDED LIKE A RABBI

Rabbi Klenicki

Once the Cardinal was invited by some group to go down to Argentina and give a talk. He asked me if I had ever heard of the group. I had, and I knew them to be a little peculiar. They were a right-wing group. This was certainly not the sort of group that had ever been particularly open or friendly towards the Jewish community. When I told him this, the Cardinal asked me whether I wouldn't come with him. So I did.

After he addressed the group, he was invited to speak at a Mass in the cathedral in Buenos Aires. I remember that in his speech, O'Connor really gave it to the people about anti-Semitism, during Mass, during the homily. He told them a Hasidic story about Jews in Poland who were taken to the woods to be killed, to be shot, and one father covers his child. So this child is saved, but when he emerges from the woods and goes to his neighbors for help, covered in blood, they tell him, "Get out, Jew." This happens a number of times. Finally, the boy appears on the doorstep of an old woman, and when she asks him who he is, he says that he is Jesus. She believes him and takes him in, and he is saved that way. It created such a reaction there.

I was watching the whole thing in the front row. I think it was strange enough for many people that a guy with a yarmulke was sitting there. At one point, the local Cardinal, who was also a friend of mine, leaned over to me and asked me if I wrote the speech. O'Connor had sounded so much like a rabbi. [Laughs.]

After the Mass, someone came over to talk to the Cardinal. He [the man] couldn't speak English, but through an interpreter, he explained that he had been a Holocaust survivor. He told O'Connor about being in Auschwitz, about the gas chambers and the suffering. All the time he talked, O'Connor held his hand, and you could tell that he was genuinely pained. It was very moving to see.

Inspiration

No matter who you are, no matter what you may have been, no matter what you fear in the future, Our Lord says, "Do not be afraid."

—*Cardinal O'Connor's Sunday homily,*
November 18, 1999

FROM HIS DAYS as a high school guidance counselor to his last years on earth, John O'Connor inspired students, colleagues, friends, and even strangers to overcome obstacles, to achieve their potential as children of God, and to summon courage in the face of tragedy and setback. He did it with words and actions, and by his example as a man who believed that people of faith had nothing to fear.

AN ANGEL ON HIS SHOULDER

James McHugh grew up in the blue-collar town of Chester, Pa., during and just after World War II. He lived, in his own words, like a street urchin, hanging out with gamblers and small-time hoods, destined for a life of petty crime, hard times, and an early grave. His mother, a single parent, decided to enroll young Jimmy in St. James High School. His guidance counselor at St. James was a young priest named Father John O'Connor.

I didn't have a father. I was a street kid in Chester. My mother was never home—she was working in the mills. And I was out there running errands for gamblers. I stole ration stamps during the war, too, and I was dealing cards in mob gambling places when I was 13 or 14 years old. If I was hungry and didn't have anything to eat, maybe I'd break into a dairy and get some milk. That was my life.

I remember this one guy with connections—he gave me a big 10-pound ham. You couldn't buy ham during World War II. He said, "Bring this home to your mother for Christmas." I did, and she said, "Where'd you get that? Get it out of this house!" So I took it out and sold it for 40 bucks.

I was in public school, but my mother took me to St. James High School for the discipline. I had a high IQ, but academically, I didn't know anything. I never studied. I didn't know the structures of sentences.

When I got to St. James, the priests scared the hell out of me. They put me in with the smart kids. My family had no money, so in my senior year, I was getting ready to go to work in the shipyard. Then one day Father O'Connor calls me into his office. He was the guidance counselor then. He said, "I was looking over the college applications. Everybody in your class is going to college except you. Why not?"

I said, "Our family doesn't have any money." I mean, college never came across my radar screen.

He said, "If I can help you out, if I get you into a school and get financial help and a job, are you willing to try college? Your IQ is so high, it might be the highest in the class, and I don't want to see that wasted if I can help it. So, are you willing to try?"

I said, "Yeah, sure. I'm not afraid."

He called a priest at Xavier University in Cincinnati and hooked me up with a deal. I could pay tuition over time, I wouldn't have to pay an entrance fee, and he got me a job. I said, "What do I have to do?" And he said, "You don't have to do anything. Just show up and pay your bills. And I'm going to tell you something, Jimmy. Once you realize the value of an education, you're never going to stop."

So I got on a Greyhound bus to Cincinnati with 20 bucks in my pocket. I worked day and night, I did some boxing to earn some money, and I made the dean's list. I really woke up and studied. Then I figured: I'm pretty smart—I want to go to Notre Dame. Why not reach for the stars? I contacted Notre

Dame, but at the time, they didn't take transfers. So I wrote back and got a priest to send them my grades, and they said, "Your grades are so high, we'll accept you." So I went to Notre Dame, and worked on the railroad and dug ditches to pay the bills. I had one of the top averages when I graduated in 1954 and went to Fordham Law and I've been practicing law now for 43 years. I've won a lot of cases all over the country. I've had a lot of positives in my life, and it all goes back to Father O'-Connor. This guy has been an angel on my shoulder for 50 years. I'm married, with a wonderful wife, and one of my daughters graduated from St. Joseph's College in Philadelphia, and another from Notre Dame, and my son's a lawyer who just bought a ranch out west. It's amazing. I'd have been nothing without this guy—he took my whole life and changed it. He showed so much love for me. It just struck me recently that I didn't speak English at the time I met him. I spoke hate. And when I think back, and I realize what this man did for me, how much love he showed, and how he turned me around.

To be honest with you, it wasn't until about 10 years ago that I gave this any thought. I was busy raising a family and trying cases. Somebody asked me, "Was there anything that really inspired you?" And those words of his came back to me: "You're never going to stop." He was right. I started to feel badly because I never bothered to thank Father O'Connor. My conscience started to bother me, and I wrote him a letter and said, "If you're ever up for sainthood, you can count me as one of your miracles." [Laughs]

Then, when I heard he was sick, I called him, and I got a call back from one of his secretaries, who said he couldn't talk to me, but he remembered me. She said he smiled when she mentioned my name. That was good enough for me.

I've always felt like there was some force propelling me. I don't know where it comes from, but I attribute it to him, because he's my only contact with the big guy upstairs.

Back then, everybody put me down, because I was a street kid. But I could feel this love from him—it was like he was saying, "Sit down, Jimmy, I'm going to take care of you." I still feel it today.

I've had a lot of good things happen to me, and now, if people come to me and need my help, I don't turn them away. I'm carrying his torch. I'm trying to give back what he gave to me. That little visit to his office way back when really paid some dividends in love and understanding. This man was a living saint, believe me.

MY FRIEND, THE CARDINAL

Sandi Merle

I think the real turning point for me was in 1995. I had triple bypass surgery which was fine except they couldn't get me off life support for eight days, rather than the 12 hours they hoped for. And when I did get off life support, they kept me in the hospital for another week and a half. On the day before I was supposed to leave, I felt a little lump in my left leg. They found something, and they were able to dissolve it. But I had to stay an extra day in the hospital. And when that day came, as I was preparing to go to my mother's home to recuperate, I had a near-death experience. I just remember saying to this lovely young nurse, whom I frightened terribly, "I'm going. Now." And all I remember—most people remember bright lights—all I remember was the color black, and then nothing. The next thing I knew there were 13 medical personnel working on me, and they told me that they had brought me back with a defibrillator. They asked me if I remembered the second incident, which I did not. They brought me back from that one, too, and later they implanted a defibrillator in me.

Having survived all this, I had to try to find out why it had happened. Being affiliated with the New York Board of Rabbis, you would figure, "Oh, she went to the biggest rabbi she could think of." I didn't. I went to the person who had become my best teacher. I called the Cardinal, and he knew, of course, how ill I had been. I said, "I have to meet with you."

You know, later on the doctors told me I always had a smile on my face. They said, "You never asked, 'why me, why me,'" which is what a young grandmother might say. I said, "You weren't there when I asked, why me?" And this wonderful doctor, Thomas Malloy, said, "What do you mean?" And I said, "When I came out of the defibrillator implantation, it was then that I said to God, 'OK, why me? Why did you bring me back? Why did you choose to spare me?' That's when I felt I had to meet with the Cardinal. And he understood full well. I asked him, "What does this mean? The answer can't be a simple one, like, 'You have children and grandchildren, you still have a mother. They still need you, and God saw that.'" I said, "No, it can't be that, because many people can say that. Everyone I know can say practically the same thing. So it has to be more."

And he said to me, "Well, what do you think it means?" I said, "It's about life, isn't it?" He knew that I am named after a very young woman, Shaina, who died in the Shoah [the Hebrew name for the Holocaust] in Treblinka. I have always been connected to her in one way or another. A lot of what I do to defend life has to do with the fact that Shaina tried very hard to defend life. She made it through the Warsaw uprising, only to die a more horrible death in the concentration camps. But she was a fighter. And so I have been one, too, all my life. And I know there's a part of her that's inside of me. And the Cardinal said, "You're right. And what I suggest that you do is do everything that you're doing now, but louder. Shout it, Sandi, and if they shout you down, shout louder."

It could have only been that man, because I respected him so, loved him so, it could have only been that man to whom I would listen. He knew there is a reason for everything. He coined a phrase—God-incidence. When I would say to him, "There is no such thing as a coincidence," he would say, "It's God-incidence." It was a very tearful session when we met, except for one laugh I gave him. Having the defibrillator implanted gives you the feeling, at least until you get used to it, that you're falling backwards. So when I walked into the residence, he stood up and pointed to a chair next to the couch. It was a rocking chair! And I wouldn't hurt him for the world. I would die first. So certainly I wasn't going to decline that chair. I sat on the edge of the chair for almost two hours, really afraid to sit back. Finally, he said to me, "Are you uncomfortable here?" And I said, "Of course not. I'm always comfortable here." And he said, "But you haven't relaxed." Then I told him that story. He threw his head back and laughed. I felt the whole episode had been worth it just to see that reaction.

He was very good to my family. I have a 12-year-old grandniece named Rachel, who lives in California. At the age of eight, Rachel was found to have an aneurysm on her brain. The arteries in the brain are so narrow that it was determined that Rachel cannot even receive surgical treatment until she is approximately 15.

I went to my friend the Cardinal to help me get through this. He started corresponding with Rachel to the point where she demanded that her parents bring her to New York to meet him. That was just before he became sick—July of 1999. You would think, "What do these two people have in common that they had something to talk about for an hour and a half." But she's a bright child, a particularly gifted child, and they had so much to talk about. He gave her his seal, with his ecclesiastical motto, "There can be no love without justice," and he gave her—thank you very much, my dear Cardinal [laughs]—a replica of the Statue of Liberty that was so big we couldn't carry it. And he gave her mom a kiddush cup, the cup that one uses on Friday night when the prayer is made over the wine.

When he became ill, Rachel wrote him a letter. She wrote many, but this particular one said, "I always knew that we were connected at the heart, but I never knew that one day we would be connected at the brain, too." And you know, it put him away, but he loved it.

RACHEL

Twelve-year-old Rachel Fader, a student at Holmes Junior High School in Davis, Calif., is Sandi Merle's grandniece. Like Sandi, she is Jewish. Rachel was diagnosed with a brain aneurysm in June of 1998.

The Cardinal and I were writing for a while, about a year and a half, from September, 1998, until he died. I wrote most of my letters on the computer because I thought that would be more formal. They were very sweet letters, the ones he wrote. He would always begin by saying it was wonderful to hear from me. I think he was hard on himself, because in one letter he thanks me for being patient with him because he hadn't answered my letter. He explained that he had to travel to Rome and elsewhere, as if I was more important than his travels to Rome to meet with people.

We went to New York to see him. We were in his office, waiting, and then I heard a voice from outside the office saying, "I hear there's somebody name Rachel waiting for me in the other room." And I knew it was him. He came in and saw me and hugged me for such a long time. He brought me over to the window and he was pointing out all the things you could see from the window—the Chrysler Building and other buildings. He asked me how school was, and what I was doing in extracurricular activities. He spent over an hour with us, and that was so surprising, you know? It was wonderful talking to him, and he was such a wonderful person.

He seemed so happy to see me, and I was so happy to see him. I loved being in that room and talking to him because he was a great listener. It was a wonderful experience.

Before we left, he gave my mom a really beautiful kiddush cup. And he gave me a replica of the Statue of Libery and a medallion with his coat of arms on it. I have it in my room now. It's in a red velvet case.

He was an inspiration to me. When he had cancer, and he was fighting it, he was just the same wonderful person he always was, even at a time when he knew he was in pretty serious condition. I didn't get to meet him again, unfortunately, but my Aunt Sandi would tell me how he was doing, that he was the same person, he just looked different and seemed tired. But he had the same spirit and was always so sweet. I thought that was wonderful, that he knew he was in a serious condition, but he acted the same way he always did and was the same person he always was.

I wrote him a letter about how great it was that two people from two different religions could be such wonderful friends and share so many things in common. I had thought, since he is a Cardinal very involved in his religion, I thought maybe we would have a lot of differences. But it actually turned out that I learned a lot about the things that Jews and Christians have in common. And from being with him I learned not just the technical religion stuff, but about people interacting with each other. I think that was pretty nice.

I think about him often. I think about the time we had together, and I replay scenes in my mind from when we met. Sometimes it makes me sad, but he's not gone from me. He may have left the world, but he didn't leave me. I have a picture of him on my desk, and I look at it often and I think about him. Sometimes, you know, when I'm having a bad day, I talk to him and he'll help me through it.

I STILL FEEL HIS PRESENCE

Ellen Cohen is Rachel's mom.

Rachel was just a little girl when they started writing to each other, and I'm sure she didn't understand the big picture, who he was and all of that. Nobody suggested that she write to him. She did it on her own. The letters she got back made a big impression on her. The tone was always so sweet and familiar, even from the beginning. Her letters touched him, too, I think. I hope they added something for him.

I wrote several letters of my own, thanking him for the Mass he said for Rachel and for showing such interest in her. Eventually, I wrote to him about something I thought he might want to know about me. My father is my Aunt Sandi's brother. They come from an Orthodox Jewish family. He married my mother, who comes from an Irish-Catholic family. My parents divorced when I was two, and I was raised Catholic and went to Catholic school until 10th grade, and later converted to Judaism. I thought he should know that. I wrote to him about that, and in response, he wrote a beautiful letter of acceptance to me, and ended with him saying that he understood that this is something I thought that God wanted for me, and the best thing I could do is be the best Jew I could be.

It was very memorable when we met him. He just had so much love in his eyes when he walked into the room and scooped Rachel up. It was as if they had known each other for a long time. Out of the blue—I certainly didn't expect this to happen—I became tearful. It was very powerful. He was talking to Rachel, asking her questions. I know she was nervous, and she was doing her best to respond. He took her over to the window and pointed out the city. Before he walked back with her to the sofa where we were sitting, he gave her this Statue of Liberty, which was no small gift. It was hard to carry, and beautiful. And then, unexpectedly, he gave me a box, and inside—and this was very much connected to the letter I sent to him—was the most beautful kiddush cup. I unwrapped it there, and I was kind of overwhelmed. I still keep it in that gold foil paper. It was a very powerful visit. I think he knew that he was ill. He didn't know how long he had, but I think he knew. I think he knew there was a special connection between him and Rachel.

It was quite a remarkable experience in our lives. I'm getting tearful. He offered a lot of support when Rachel was first diagnosed. It was a really, really difficult time. I took comfort in knowing we had a connection with him. I was very naive about things. I had no idea really who this man was. And he became really important to us, so much so that when he died, I selfishly was focused on my loss. I thought, "Who would I be able to write to about her?" It was quite an emotional and spiritual experience for us.

He had such a presence. It came from the heart. He was a refuge. He really was a refuge for us. I still feel his presence, and I know he will always be with us.

THE CHURCH IS THE CHURCH

Archbishop Harry Flynn of St. Paul was a parish priest in the mid-1980s when he had his most memorable encounter with Cardinal O'Connor.

In April of 1986, on a Monday, I received a call from the Papal Nuncio, Archbiship Pio Laghi. He asked me to come to Washington. I went on Thursday of that week, and he told me that I had been appointed Bishop in Lafayette, Louisiana. I don't think I was able to grasp what he was saying in the brevity of that meeting. I returned to Latham [in upstate New York] that afternoon and was becoming more and more convinced that I should not accept this appointment as bishop in Lafayette.

At that time, my brother was very ill and his wife was in a nursing home. The last of my aunts, who had brought me up, was also in a nursing home, and I bore some responsibility for all of them. I returned to my parish, St. Ambrose, and I became convinced that I should not accept the appointment.

On Tuesday of the following week, I typed a letter indicating that I could not possibly accept this appointment and that I really did not want to be a bishop, but to live my life as a pastor, specifically, pastor of St. Ambrose parish. I skillfully chose the proper words so that the letter would be very respectful but at the same time, very firm. I sent the letter on a Wednesday, via Federal Express, to the Nunciature in Washington. I knew that it would arrive on Thursday, so, on Thursday morning, I went to my home in Schroon Lake in the Adirondack Mountains. It was a beautiful April day. I recall that later in the morning, the phone at the cottage rang quite frequently—it rarely rang at other times. I didn't answer the phone and had a rather quiet afternoon enjoying the beauty of the mountains and the scenery of the lake.

That evening, I was in the kitchen preparing dinner for myself, and a knock came on the back door. I opened the door, and it was a New York State trooper. He said to me, "Are you Father Flynn?" I responded that I was.

He then said, "Cardinal O'Connor wants you to call him tonight, and here is the number."

I don't think I finished preparing that supper. I went in and called the Cardinal's residence. I identified myself and he said, "I would like to see you in my office tomorrow. Come any time." I locked up the cabin and returned to my rectory in Latham. Then, on Friday morning, I took the train down to New York City and went to the Cardinal's office. Once there, he asked me to explain why I had sent the letter to Archbishop Laghi. I told him the many reasons why I did not feel I could accept the appointment. I went through the long list of family obligations, the fact that I has been at St. Ambrose only five years, and that, frankly, I did not really want to be a bishop. I had lived with the Bishop of Albany for two years and saw, at times, the misunderstandings that came his way.

The Cardinal listened intently. He never interupted me. When I stopped talking, he said, "Are you finished?" I told him I was.

And then he said, "Harry, the Church is the Church. You do what the Church wants."

I'll never forget that moment. It seemed as though a tremendous burden had been lifted from my shoulders. I suppose having the opportunity of talking about what was deepest in my heart gave me an opportunity for a complete catharsis.

Then, the Cardinal said to me, "Will you accept?"

I responded that I would. He pointed to the phone and told me to call Archbishop Laghi, which I did. The rest is history.

HE CALLED ME JOHNNY

The Rev. John Higgins of Holy Rosary parish in the Bronx was a teenager when Cardinal O'Connor arrived in New York. After graduation from Thomas Aquinas College in California, he went to work for a group called Catholics United for the Faith.

It was 1990, and I was 21 years old and had just returned from a business trip in Dallas. My parish, St. Joseph's in Millbrook [upstate New York] was celebrating its 100th anniversary. My mom is the organist at the church, and Cardinal O'Connor was the principal celebrant of the Mass. I got there just in time.

I had a habit of genuflecting before receiving Communion, and did so at this Mass, and I stayed in the church after the Mass to make a thanksgiving. I didn't leave the church when the rest of the parishioners left. Cardinal O'Connor said to somebody, "Bring me that young man," meaning me. That would have been his style. So somebody came back in to get me, and I was told that Cardinal O'Connor wanted to meet me. So I went outside to meet him, of course. He was still greeting parishioners. I went over to him, and he said to me, "Have you thought about becoming a priest?"

And I said, "Yes, well, I've been thinking of becoming a religious." And he said, "Why don't you study for my archdiocese?" And I said, "OK," and I did.

There were some steps along the way between that conversation and being accepted at the seminary several months later, of course, but he had extended a personal invitation to me, and I had accepted it. Gosh, I was honored and happy to be noticed by the Cardinal, and delighted that he should take an interest in me. It showed to me that he had a real interest in vocations, and that he must have been happy to be a priest if he felt called to invite others.

It also showed me that he had great insight. Why did he single me out? Yes, I showed reverence for the Eucharist, but was that enough? Perhaps he had a had a deeper sense. Maybe it was an inspiration.

He ordained me on May 11, 1996. Sometime before, I wasn't sure if he would, because he had turned 75 in 1995 and his retirement came up. Fortunately, the Holy Father saw otherwise, and I was blessed to have the Cardinal ordain me. On that day, the Cardinal gave a homily about discouragement, but I didn't feel discouraged. I don't think he was speaking from his own experience, but maybe from the experience of some of his brother priests. When priests came to him to tell him that they were leaving the priesthood, the Cardinal was always compassionate. At the end of the discussion, he would get down on his knees and ask the priest who was going to leave to give him a blessing. It would be the priest's last.

The highlight of the ceremony for me was when we were facing the altar with our backs to the people, just after being vested by our brother priests. And the Cardinal said, as he said every year, "Well, they are priests." The parents of all the new priests, including my mother and father, were sitting in the front. I could look down at my mother and father and see how deeply moved they were. The congregation was cheering—it was a tremendous moment.

He always remembered my name. He called me Johnny, which is what my parents called me.

SPIRITUAL AND SECULAR

Eileen Christian

He was an inspiration to me in both my spiritual life and my professional life. I would read everything he wrote that I was privy to, I heard many of his homilies, I saw the way he worked with his priests, with the lay people who worked with him. In both a spiritual and a secular way, it was a great lesson for me. I didn't see him on a day in and day out basis, so, no, I didn't see him getting frustrated or annoyed. But for the most part, I think I have a very good sense of the whole man. Consequently, my spiritual life spills over to my secular life. I strive for that every day, and I learned that from him. I kick myself when I feel as though I'm not living up to what he taught. He advised me from the time that I was a kid—he said you have to actualize your potential, the potential that God has given you, and you have to listen to that.

A TRULY MORAL PERSON

Howard Rubenstein

He periodically invited me to breakfast at his residence. I loved it. I found that he enriched my life by having me read more about Catholicism, and having a greater understanding of his devotion not only to his community, but to

John O'Connor as a student at Tilden Junior H.S. in Philadelphia.
(Courtesy of Sandi Merle)

The future cardinal entered St. Charles Borromeo Seminary as a teenager. He remained in touch with the young men he met there, and hosted a dinner for them several months before he died.
(Courtesy of Sandi Merle)

As Cardinal Archbishop of New York, O'Connor became a leader of the worldwide Catholic Church. He traveled to Ethiopia in 1987 to call attention to the war-torn nation's famine.

(Credit: Chris Sheridan/*Catholic New York*)

With his friend Ed Koch, Cardinal O'Connor traveled to Ireland in 1988 to pray for peace and justice in Northern Ireland. With the Mayor and Cardinal is the late Tomas Cardinal O Fiaich, then Archbishop of Armagh.

Father John O'Connor offers Mass aboard the U.S.S. Canberra in 1962.

To the occasional dismay of his fellow administrators, Cardinal O'Connor was intensely pro-union. The hat he is wearing bears the logo of Local 1199 of the hospital workers union, led by his friend Dennis Rivera.
(Credit: Chris Sheridan/ *Catholic New York*)

On Pentecost Sunday, Cardinal O'Connor administered the sacrament of Confirmation to disabled children. Afterwards, he met the families and offered encouragement to them.
(Credit: Chris Sheridan/ *Catholic New York*)

In the early 1990s, Cardinal O'Connor led a pro-life march to an abortion clinic in midtown Manhattan. The city's Police Department fitted him with a bulletproof vest for the march.
(Credit: Chris Sheridan/ *Catholic New York*)

Even in bad weather, Cardinal O'Connor never missed a St. Patrick's Day parade.

(Credit: Chris Sheridan/ *Catholic New York*)

Pope John Paul II and
Cardinal O'Connor enjoyed a
close relationship, made more
intimate during the Pope's visit
to New York in 1995.
(Credit:Chris Sheridan/
Catholic New York)

Cardinal O'Connor sought to
reconcile centuries of distrust
between Catholics and Jews.
Here, he prays at the
Wailing Wall in Jerusalem.
(Credit: Chris Sheridan/
Catholic New York)

Mary Ward (left), the Cardinal's sister,
and Eileen Christian (right), his niece,
bid farewell to their brother,
uncle and spiritual advisor.
(Credit: Chris Sheridan/ *Catholic New York*)

His pilgrimage over, John Cardinal O'Connor
is taken to his final resting place in the crypt
beneath the main altar of St. Patrick's Cathedral.
(Credit:Chris Sheridan/ *Catholic New York*)

the larger community. He was really devoted to New York. And he made a number of speeches about Catholicism having its roots in the Jewish religion. I must have heard him give speeches like that five or six times. So, I will always remember him with great affection and kindness.

He had an impact on my thinking and how I conduct myself. He truly was a moral person who did not cut corners, who stuck up for what he believed. I didn't find him saying, "Let's make a deal." He'd say, "Let's do what is right." I think about him because any community—Jewish, Muslim, any of the communities—would do well to see how he conducted his life. It has to do with his attitude towards people.

I'm a better person just by knowing him. There's only a handful of people I can say that about.

SHINE YOUR LIGHT

Jennifer Lynch

The Inner City Scholarship Fund had a program called "Be a Student's Friend," where we would pair up contributors who gave $2,000 to the fund with individual students from the Catholic schools. Twice a year we had ceremonies in the Cathedral where sponsors would meet the students. There was a ceremony called "Shine Your Light," where patrons had a candle, and would light their students' candle in the chapel. Then we'd go to the residence for a reception. The Cardinal always let us use the residence—he often would stop by, do his thing, and then go upstairs. Even when he was sick, he allowed us to use the residence for our events.

I remember one reception where we had lots of kids—a lot more than we ever had before. They were all sugared up, too, from the cookies we provided, and they were a little rowdy. I remember thinking, "I'm going to get reamed about this." I was thinking we'd never get a chance to use the residence again. The Cardinal could have run upstairs, but he made a point of meeting all the patrons and spending a lot of time with the kids, much more than you would have ever expected. It was neat, watching him with the kids, because he usually was so serious. Some of the kids had left juice cups lying around, and all I could think of was, "Please don't spill anything." But that seemed to be the furthest thing from the Cardinal's mind.

THE RIGHT THING TO DO

Eileen White

I have never known to this day anybody who worked as hard at being a priest, a CEO, a person. When you work with somebody who inspires you, that's where you want to be, and he inspired me. And I liked him. I thought he was a lot of fun. For me, it was one of those great gifts, this job. It didn't have any parameters. He allowed me to take it as far as I wanted it to go. We worked on books together, he did a television program for a while that I worked on with him, I wrote speeches for him, and I worked with him on establishing the Sisters of Life. All of these things made my job seem right. I'm a person of faith, and I think that's where God wanted me to be.

Throughout my years with him, from time to time we'd have an intense conversation about whether I should continue to be there. I was young, I was a lawyer, I had a great future in front of me, and the Cardinal was concerned. He was concerned that the Church couldn't pay me what I'd be making in the open market. Was I in any way going to hinder myself when this job ended? And we always came to the same conclusion, that this was where I was supposed to be.

Compassion

Mine is the theology of suffering.
—*Cardinal O'Connor, quoted by Nat Hentoff*

JOHN O'CONNOR UNDERSTOOD suffering. He had witnessed it, and had experienced it first-hand. Because he saw a human face where others might see a general social problem, because he saw the person who suffered, and not just the suffering itself, John O'Connor opened his heart to those who needed his love the most: the weak, the ill, the desperate, the poor in spirit, the anguished. In their suffering, he saw the suffering of Christ.

"I HAVEN'T FORGOTTEN"

As a religion writer for The New York Times, *Ari Goldman covered Cardinal O'Connor from 1983 to 1993. His relationship with the Cardinal was not unlike that of most reporters and their subjects—there were times of intimacy and times of estrangement. Mr. Goldman, author of* The Search for God at Harvard *and* Being Jewish, *is now a professor of journalism at Columbia University.*

We hit it off from the beginning. I'm an Orthodox Jew and I think he felt that he had found a kindred spirit. I took his religion seriously, and the Cardinal appreciated that.

On the eve of his coming to New York, he made a statement comparing abortion to the Holocaust. He talked about being in Dachau and thinking about aborted babies. This was right before he left Scranton. It was barely reported in the papers, but the *Times* editorialized against this comparison. It really slammed him.

I called him up and asked if he had seen the editorial. He was wounded by it. He needed to talk about it and explain that he didn't mean to offend people. I let him have his say in a follow-up article. He loved me for that article, because it gave him a chance to present himself clearly. I think he saw me as an ally.

During my first year of covering him, I had a lot of access. I called him on his private line. After about a year, I was assigned to do a magazine article on him for the *Times*. I wrote a tough piece. It's one thing to be a daily journalist and write what he says, but it's another thing to probe deeper, to talk to a person's enemies. I lost access after that. All the good will I had built up had dissipated. Eventually we recovered, but it was never the same.

In 1995, my mother was in last stages of battling cancer. She was in Sloan Kettering [Cancer Center], where they were aggressively treating her, but it became clear there was nothing more they could do. My stepfather and my brother and I looked for the best place for her, and it turned out to be a Catholic hospice in the Bronx called Calvary. We learned that Jews are good at keeping people alive through aggressive treatment—that they knew how to save sick people—but that Catholics were good at providing for the dying. We were an Orthodox family and wanted her in a Jewish environment, but nothing came close to Calvary Hospital, run by the Archdiocese of New York.

Before bringing my mother there, we wanted to make sure she would be in a comfortable environment. We met with social workers and other staff, who arranged for the crucifix to be taken down in my mother's room and provided kosher food. We were a family in crisis, and it was like the whole hospital was turned over inside out for my mother's comfort. The medical director greeted us at the door and saw my mother to her room.

A few days later, I was in a quiet moment with the medical

director, and I said, "This is the most amazing facility I've ever seen. My mother is as comfortable as she could be."

And he smiled and said, "It's not every day that the Cardinal calls."

That blew me away. There are 17 Catholic hospitals with something like 1,300 beds in the Archdiocese of New York. And Cardinal O'Connor knew that Ari Goldman's mother was moving into one of those beds in the Bronx.

To this day I don't know how he knew about my mother. I called his secretary, Monsignor [James] McCarthy, and said, "How did you know?" And he said, "The Cardinal knows what's going on."

Six months after my mother died, I got a personal note from the Cardinal. Remember, I was no longer a *Times* reporter. He had no reason to be nice to me. He owed me nothing. But I received this personal note, which I saved. The Cardinal wrote: "The loss of a parent is so hard . . . We often get a lot of attention when we lose a parent, then six months goes by, and everyone forgets, but you don't forget. I haven't forgotten either." [Pauses]. There are 2.3 million Catholics in the Archdiocese of New York, and I'm a Jew, and he writes that kind of letter to me.

MURDER ON A BEACH

James Zappalorti was a gay 45-year-old Vietnam veteran who lived with his parents in a sparsely populated corner of Staten Island in 1990. He had never been the same since Vietnam— he was troubled, and often fought with his father, a man who made stained-glass windows in a small studio near their home. On January 22, 1990, James Zappalorti was stabbed to death on a beach near a small hut he had built for himself. Police classifed the murder as a hate crime; James Zappalorti was murdered because he was gay. Cardinal O'Connor came to the funeral Mass and continued to stay in touch with James Zappalorti's aging parents.

More than a decade later, Michael Zappalorti, James's elder brother, cannot speak about the murder or of Cardinal O'Connor's kindness toward the family without his eyes filling with tears. He now runs the family stained-glass business, and plans one day to memorialize the Cardinal in a piece of art. Outside his small studio is a slender tree, and next to it is a plaque placed there by a local civic group in memory of his brother. Cardinal O'Connor was present for the plaque's unveiling.

Cardinal O'Connor came to my brother's funeral Mass, and all I can say about him—[pauses] this brings back a lot of bad memories, you know—is that he was a very kind and understanding man. That's the best I can say about him. I remember him talking with my mother at the [funeral] Mass, and my mother was a very devout Catholic, and the Cardinal said to her, "I've never seen such devotion." That meant a lot.

He helped my family, that's for sure. [Pauses] What he did for my mother . . . what he did for my mother. [Pauses] He was there when we planted the tree outside. He even came down to the house to visit her when my mother was sick, you know? My father, too.

I remember coming into my parents' house and saying, "I found him dead on the beach." My father and mother, I'll never forget the look on their faces. I said, "They killed him," and the two of them broke down and cried. I'll never forget that look as long as I live, and I've been living with it ever since. I don't know what to tell you. The Cardinal was a big comfort. Are you kidding me? He helped my parents a lot. I only wish I had sent him a letter, although we did thank him. What he did for my mother—he's got plenty of Heaven points for that.

Me and my brother always got along. There's not a picture of me when I was growing up where my kid brother wasn't with me. He was like my shadow. But Cardinal O'Connor— I've got nothing but good to say about that man.

❖

Monsignor Peter Finn was the Zappalortis' pastor

I got a call one morning that James Zappalorti had been found dead on the beach. I went over and I anointed him, and then I spoke with the mother and father. I had been bringing Mrs. Zappalorti Communion at home, and the father was a daily communicant. Then, of course, the story appeared in the newspaper, and I got a call from the Cardinal, who knew it had happened in my parish. He decided he was going to come down to speak with the family, especially after he heard that the mother and father were such devoted parishioners.

The family took great consolation from the Cardinal. And the Cardinal wanted to make a statement loud and clear about the reverence for all human life.

This was the kind of compassion and care he showed for anybody with a problem, whether it was priest or poet, male or female, gay or straight. If people were hurting, he would minister to them.

YOU HAVE TO HAVE FAITH

Joe Zwilling

I had a family difficulty concerning one of my siblings. I went and told him about it, and asked him to pray for us, for my parents, who were having a hard time coming to grips with this. About two weeks later, I was talking to my mom, and she said, "Thanks for having the Cardinal send a letter." I said, "What letter?" He had gotten my parents' address—how he got it I don't know, but he got it, and he wrote them, saying, "Joseph has explained to me what happened. I want you to know I said Mass for you today, and you've been in my prayers. I know you are good parents. God writes straight with crooked lines. You have to have faith that this is all going to work out." This meant a great deal to my parents. They thought at first that I had asked the Cardinal to do it. But I didn't know anything about it.

When I got married, I invited the Cardinal to my wedding, and he wrote back a nice note. He certainly gave the impression in the letter that he wasn't coming, which is what I kind of expected. So I'm in the limo going to the church with my best man and my ushers, and I see the Cardinal's secretary standing outside the church. Then I see the Cardinal. I said, "Holy cow, he's here!" I ran inside church and told my wife-to-be, "I don't want you to panic, but the Cardinal's here." Later, I went back and read the note he sent, and I noticed that he never really said he wasn't coming. I realized then that he didn't want to turn our wedding day into "Oh, the Cardinal's coming to our parish," which is exactly what would have happened. He was very sensitive to those kinds of things.

MY PASTOR

Brother Tyrone Davis

My father passed away on April 3, 1999, the day after my birthday and on his 50th wedding anniversary. During the week before the funeral, Cardinal O'Connor scheduled a meeting with the parents of Amadou Diallo [a West African immigrant killed by police who mistakenly believed they were in danger]. He asked me to be in on that meeting. It was upstairs in his office. There was no press there. It was a pastoral visit, and he sat on the sofa with Mrs. Diallo. There was a real warmth to his presence. Toward the end of that meeting, he informed Mrs. Diallo and everyone there that my father had passed away, and that he was very grateful for my being there in light of the fact that I was preparing for my father's funeral. When I left that meeting, he said to me, "I will see you on Friday." That caught me off guard. His secretary told me that the Cardinal planned to be at the funeral, which was way out in New Jersey. I knew that he had a meeting scheduled with the Papal Nuncio [the Pope's representative] that same morning. He rescheduled it, and he came to the church. The church was packed, and in walks John Cardinal O'Connor. And he went and spent some time with my mom, and then he knelt down, and he—excuse me [pauses]—and he knelt down and prayed for my father. He spoke to the congregation—he thought the Mass was going to be a little earlier than it was, so he apologized that he would have to leave.

It was such an inspiration for everyone who was in that church, and I will never forget it. Who was I that he would take two to three hours, by the time he traveled from New York to New Jersey and back again, out of his schedule? Many of the people in the church had never seen him in person before, and there he was. They were wondering who my father really was! [Laughs]

That's Cardinal O'Connor. I remember years ago telling people, "I don't see him as a pastor." And in the end, he became my pastor.

"JESUS WAS ALIVE IN HIM"

Sister Joan Curtin

When I celebrated my 25th anniversary as a sister, I asked him to say the Mass. We had it here in St. John the Evangelist [a church attached to the Catholic Center in midtown Manhattan]. There was family and some staff and colleagues. Now, my family came from Ireland—my mother, my father, my uncles. They weren't wealthy and they didn't have much of a relationship with the clergy. They went to church, but they didn't have that relationship. And after the Mass my uncle—he was tough—said to me, "The Cardinal is a very humble man." I think my uncle said that because the Cardinal could relate so well with all of my family. The Cardinal was just himself. He was very warm, and was lovely with my mother, who's never forgotten it and who eventually became a friend of his.

Another time I was called out of a staff meeting because my mother had fallen and had to be taken to the hospital. While I'm in the hospital, I got a phone call from the Cardinal as he's stepping onto the plane for Rome: "How's your mother? Tell her I'm praying for her." That's the kind of pastor he was. I think he realized the importance of his presence as a Cardinal and as a priest. And that, I think, is what makes the difference. So even though you may not have always agreed with the way he presented something—and there were plenty of us—the person came through. In public, he came off very strong, especially about the teachings of the

Church, and for some people, that was difficult. But on the personal level, if someone came to him with a problem, he would always find the time. The pastor in him always came out. Jesus was alive in him.

COMFORTING THE AFFLICTED

Ed Koch

The Cardinal was extremely important to me during the corruption crisis [in the mid-1980s, when several city politicians were found guilty of graft and other crimes]. I went into a state of what I believe was clinical depression. I couldn't discuss it with anybody or go to a pyschiatrist because nobody wants the Mayor to be perceived as nutty. [Laughs] I had it all bottled up. My fear was that people would think I was corrupt. I didn't have wealth. Whatever I did, I did because the people believed me and believed I was honest. I thought to myself, "Will the people think I'm dishonest?" I couldn't stand it. I thought of suicide. I couldn't get up in the morning. I loved my job, but I could hardly move. I was lying in bed on Sunday, and there was a call from the Cardinal, who said, "Ed, I know you feel terrible, and that you're suffering so. But everybody knows you're an honest man." Now, I had never discussed this with him. But he knew intuitively what I was going through. I was amazed. My own family didn't know. My sister said later, "Ed, why didn't you tell us?" But the Cardinal intuitively knew, and he said to me,

"There's nothing you have to worry about." I said, "Oh, Your Eminence, I can't tell you how much this call means to me." And he said, "Oh, it's nothing." And I said, "Oh, yes. The Lubbavitcher Rebbe didn't call me." So I never forgot that.

The other major occasion I recall his comfort was when [Police Officer] Steven McDonald was injured when an adolescent he was running after turned and shot him [in 1986]. He was taken to Bellevue Hospital. They called me and I went down there. I didn't know Steven McDonald. His family was there, his wife, her parents. They told me he was going to die. It was awful, just awful. [Tears are streaming from the corner of his eyes. He pauses a few seconds] I was very struck by the religiosity of the two families. They were praying. [He pauses for about five seconds.] I called the Cardinal. And I said [his voice breaks, and he pauses again]—it was a very emotional time—I said, "Your Eminence, I've never called your before under these circumstances and I don't want to disturb your rest, but there's an enormous tragedy here. And I think if you came over, you could provide comfort to this family, because [pauses] this young cop is going to die."

So he said, "I'll be right over." And he was, and of course he provided great comfort. He asked me to go with him upstairs to the officer's bedside. I don't know whether he gave him last rites or not. I didn't stay very long. But—Steven McDonald is still alive. His wife was pregnant at the time, and she later had a sweet little boy. The Cardinal christened him. And I used to see them at Midnight Mass on Christmas Eve all the time.

STEVEN McDONALD

Steven McDonald has been in a wheelchair, paralyzed from the neck down, since being shot in 1986. He literally had to learn how to breathe again. Several years later after the shooting, Mr. McDonald publicly forgave the young man who shot him, and he grieved when the assailant himself was killed in a traffic accident not long after being released from prison. Despite his disability, Mr. McDonald remains a member of the New York City Police Department, and was recently promoted to detective. He speaks to groups around the country about forgiveness and reconciliation.

On July 12, 1986, I was shot a little after four o'clock in the afternoon. I struggled through the next two days to live. That first day, Mayor Koch came in, and he was impressed, I'm told, by the faith of my wife, who was carrying my son at the time, and our other family members. Everybody was praying, and there might have been a Mass being said by the chaplain. The Mayor didn't normally do this, but he decided he should bring the Cardinal in.

Cardinal O'Connor would come quite often to Bellevue Hospital. I was there for 10 months, and then I went away to a hospital in Denver for another seven or eight months. He would check on my progress and he would offer Mass in the hospital room. The biggest occasion was the first anniversary of our wedding, on November 9. He did that Mass.

The Cardinal would talk to me about the value of my suffering, and the suffering of Christ on the cross, and how it would help other people. A funny side story—a few years later, probably the late 1980s or early 1990s—we were at a reception in the Cardinal's residence after the Midnight Mass. He struck up a conversation with me. I told him that I had been a Navy corpsman and had been stationed in the Brooklyn Navy Yard in October of 1979, when the Holy Father came to New York for the first time. I knew that the military vicariate was in Manhattan, and I called over there and pretended to be the religious petty officer for the Brooklyn Navy Yard. I asked them for tickets for the Mass at Yankee Stadium. This was all a big lie, of course. There is no such title, but I was just making this up so I could get my hands on a few tickets. I wanted to take the people I worked with and my parents.

I was telling him how I got the tickets and that I went to the Mass and it was a great experience. The Cardinal was smiling the whole time. Then he kind of whispered in my ear. He said, "Steven, I don't know if you know this, but that was my office at the time [the military vicariate], and those were my people you lied to to get those tickets." We both looked at each other, and I was a little embarrassed. But he laughed.

Six years ago, I was contemplating suicide. I talked to Patti Ann [his wife] about it. I was having a difficult time. She called the Cardinal—it was a spring or summer afternoon, and I believe it was on a weekend. She called the residence and talked to the Cardinal, and he was at the house in 90 minutes. He spent the afternoon counseling Patti Ann and me. I didn't know if I was praying right, if God was listening to what I was praying for. I was struggling with that. I remember him saying to me that my life was a prayer, and that God is always listening to our prayers. I learned later that prayer is something we do in our time, and the answers come in God's time.

He would call at night frequently to see how we were doing. Patti Ann would call him and bare her soul. They were good friends. He was always a great priest—a real example of faith. He helped me in so many ways.

The Midnight Masses we attended were faith-filled experiences. I was just watching a tape of the 1998 Midnight Mass, when our son, Conor, was an altar server. Conor held the Cardinal's miter during the Mass, and the Cardinal said some very nice things about us. His homily was very personal, and he spoke in such a tone of voice that he set you off in the right direction after you left Mass.

For the longest time, Patti Ann and I would go to the 10:15 Mass on Sunday, which the Cardinal celebrated. One Mass sticks out in my mind. It was December of 1989. Patti Ann and I showed up, and everything struck us as unusual and alarming. Mayor Koch was in the front pew. The Police Commissioner, Richard Condon, was pacing about, and there were police officers everywhere. I said, "What the heck is going on here?" Nobody would tell us. Then, somebody said that there was going to be a demonstration during Mass.

Then, during the distribution of Communion, somebody started yelling, then a second person, then a third, then 10 other people. They were cursing. It was ACT-UP, the gay-rights organization. Patti Ann jumped behind me, and afterwards I had to laugh—like I was going to protect her, here I am strapped down in my chair. It was the most frightening thing we had experienced since the shooting. You could feel the presence of evil in the church that day. I think everybody in the Cathedral was frightened.

The Cardinal came from behind the altar and he stepped forward to the top steps. And he just started praying. He didn't shout out orders to the Mayor or the police officers. He just started praying. All this confusion and violence and evil was going on, and here was an example of Christ-like behavior. That's what the Cardinal's example was to us. I thought it was the most profound experience I had ever witnessed.

My cousin, Michael Ferris, had AIDS and was dying in New York-Cornell Hospital. Toward the end of his life, in early 1991, I called the Cardinal at the request of my aunt and uncle to see if he would visit my cousin. He went a number of times to bring him Communion and to talk and pray. At the end of Michael's life, in the last few hours when Michael was straining to breathe, do you know what he had in his hand? He was holding the prayer book the Cardinal gave to him. One of the nurses said he always talked about the Cardinal and how he came to bring him Communion. It was an example of the kind of love that the Cardinal passed on to people. You can't make up that stuff.

The Cardinal was like a grandfather to Conor. At a very young age, Conor is a very committed Catholic. Conor had his first Holy Communion and his Confirmation with the Cardinal. This past January [2001], a few months after the Cardinal died, Conor, Patti Ann, and I were asked to do a reading at a jubilee concert in St. Patrick's Cathedral for the disabled. The reading was on the life of Beethoven. While we were waiting to go on the altar, we were surrounded by well-wishers and friends, people we knew and people we didn't know. I lost track of Conor, so I looked around quickly, and there he was, on the kneeler behind the crypt. He was there for a minute or two. When he was finished, I asked him what he was doing. He said he was talking, and praying, to Cardinal O'Connor.

Patti Ann McDonald

Steven was injured on a Saturday, and that Sunday, a police officer drove me back to the hospital after I went home to get some rest. We heard over his radio that Cardinal O'Connor and Mayor Koch were going to the hospital. Steven thought Ed Koch was a great mayor, and we had already talked months before about wanting to go to one of Cardinal O'Connor's Masses. When I went up to see Steven, he mouthed some words to me, which basically were, "Can you believe who came to see me today?"

Later on that day, the Cardinal said he would offer Mass the following day, Monday, for Steven. So I told everybody from our families that we had to go to St. Patrick's the next day for the Mass. What the Cardinal meant was that he would say Mass for Steven wherever he was scheduled to be the next day, but I misunderstood. The Cardinal was notified about the confusion, and he then invited us to Mass in his residence the next day.

As time went on, the Cardinal visited the hospital regularly, and he'd call me to see how Steven was doing. We developed a close relationship—he had a niece [Eileen Ward Christian] who was similar in age, and I think that was part of our relationship.

He gave me the number of his private line, and while I didn't abuse the privilege, I did call him, and he was there for me. I found I could speak to him about anything. When I sat down and had some heavy conversations with him, he would reassure me. He'd tell me that whatever I was feeling was OK, that I should hold on and stay strong and to offer up our suffering to relieve the suffering of others. He had a Christ-like way of touching people. He helped us realize that we could have a life, and he helped us work though our ups and downs. Marriage is difficult enough sometimes, and with Steven injured, well, he just knew the right things to say. He helped strengthen Steven and me.

Conor McDonald is a student at Chaminade High School on Long Island.

The Cardinal was really there for my mom and dad. When I was a kid, I didn't see him as this important person. It was like he was a family friend, like a grandfather. When I was a baby, I used to stay in his residence. Once, the Cardinal was talking to a reporter and saying that nobody was allowed to touch a certain chair, and then they see this little kid coming around and touching it. And the housekeeper, Maura O'Kelly, said, "He's the only one who can touch it." And the baby was me.

My dad read the Cardinal's articles in *Catholic New York*, and he listened to what the Cardinal said. On pro-life, that's a big thing with our family. I'm passionate about pro-life, including being against capital punishment. I'm pro-life all the way—life is what it's all about.

I'm so happy to say that I knew Cardinal O'Connor. He told me to keep the faith about my dad, and to be strong. All that inspirational stuff. I was lucky that my dad was paralyzed when I was born, because I could never have coped with it if I was born for like five years and all of a sudden my dad's in a wheelchair.

When Cardinal O'Connor helped out my mom and my dad, he helped me out. Now that he's up there with God, he's probably taking care of a lot of people, hopefully us too, and he's helping my dad. We pray to him that he'll help my dad somehow get up from his chair someday.

Steven McDonald

We've seen God in our lives so often, it would take hours to talk about how many times He has intervened. And I don't think it was a coincidence that Conor was up there at that Midnight Mass holding Cardinal O'Connor's miter. I wouldn't be surprised if one day Conor was a priest in the New York Archdiocese. It would be a storybook scenario if Conor followed in the Cardinal's footsteps. He may go ahead and prove me wrong, but I have a strong feeling that that's where Conor's life is taking him.

TEARS FOR HIS NEPHEW

Eileen Christian's brother John Ward, the Cardinal's nephew, died of cancer in 1997.

The first day that John was diagnosed, he immediately had surgery scheduled. I was supposed to drive to Manhattan from my job to pick up my uncle, and we were scheduled to leave at a certain time so we could be at the hospital in Philadelphia when John was expected out of surgery. Hours before I was supposed to leave, my uncle called and said, "You have to come now. The surgery couldn't happen. They opened him up and closed him up right away." We drove there and back. Monsignor Gerald Walsh, my uncle's secretary, was with us and he did all the driving. I remember saying to my uncle when we got back to New York, "How can you be so stoic?" And he said, "I'm the only one in this family who has to be stoic. Somebody has to be." And then he said, "When I got that phone call today, I went into my chapel and cried. I spent 20 minutes praying the Rosary and cried the whole time."

"HE MADE IT RIGHT"

Monsignor Bergin

One time, a child in the care of a nanny in Westchester died, and she was held responsible. A couple of priests came forward as character witnesses for the nanny, which greatly upset the parents and grandparents of the child. They contacted the Cardinal and demanded to know how priests could do such a thing. The Cardinal took a personal interest in the family, and tried to help them deal with their grief and bitterness.

One night, we're on our way to a meeting at Archbishop Stepinac High School in White Plains. As we're leaving to go up there, the Cardinal says, "Remind me that there's a wake I want to go to on the way back." The grandmother of the poor child had died, and the family had called the Cardinal on his way out the door. He throws a cell phone to me in the back of the car and asks me to find out where the wake is. We know the family lives in St. Joseph's parish in Bronxville, but we don't know the funeral home. We call the parish, and the pastor's not there. Nobody at the rectory can help us. The Cardinal grabs the phone, but we're getting nothing.

We get to the meeting, and I go through the phone book and call around until we find out where the wake is. The meeting ends at about five minutes to nine, and wakes always end at nine o'clock. The Cardinal gets on the phone to tell the people at the funeral home that we're on our way, to keep the family there, we'll be there in 10 minutes. Some kid on the other end says, "Sorry, we're closing." The Cardinal says, "This is Cardinal O'Connor." The kid says, "Sorry, we're closing." So the Cardinal asks to talk to the manager, and he gets him on the phone. The manager apologizes and says he'll let the family know. We get there about 10 after 9. And he comforts the relatives, and they're getting teary-eyed, and so is he. And all of the bitterness and all of the anger they felt about the priests who were character witnesses for the nanny is gone. That's the kind of quiet pastoral work he did, and few people knew about it. He made it right. He made it right.

BEYOND WHAT WAS NECESSARY

As chairman and chief executive officer of Goldman, Sachs, Jon Corzine was one of the leading patrons of the Inner City Scholarship Fund. Mr. Corzine, who is not Catholic, worked closely with Cardinal O'Connor through the Fund. In the fall of 2000, Mr. Corzine was named to receive an award from the Scholarship Fund in recognition of his largely unknown work on behalf of poor Catholic school students. At the time, he also was the Democratic candidate for the U.S. Senate from New Jersey, and had adopted the party's pro-choice position on abortion rights. As a controversy loomed, Mr. Corzine quietly withdrew as an honoree.

I dealt with Cardinal O'Connor on educational issues and the parochial schools, and he was absolutely dedicated to making sure that the kids he was responsible for had an opportunity to have a quality education in more than just schoolhouse terms, but in their lives in general. It was his ministry—to make sure that kids have the tools, morally as well as educationally. In any discussion I ever had with him about the schools, I came away with the motivation to do more, to participate more, in the program.

I'll never forget the kindness he showed me personally when we had a clash with some parts of the greater Catholic community when I was going to get an award for supporting the Inner City Scholarship Fund. My political stands and his views in regard to issues of choice were different. But he went out of his way to reach out and contact me during this awkward time. And in no way was there a compromise with regard to his views. It gave me a whole different perspective on his faith and his beliefs. It was remarkable how gracious he was. I thought he went way beyond what was necessary to make me feel comfortable. And not in any sense did this compromise his views on core issues.

HE NEVER SAID NO

Raymond C. Teatum is first deputy to the City Clerk of New York. He is on the Board of Trustees at St. Clare's Hospital, head of the honorary ushers at St. Patrick's Cathedral, and is a Knight of Malta.

We [the honorary ushers] used to serve his Mass in the morning in the Cathedral, and he'd always ask about my wife, who adored him. My answer always was: "Your Eminence, how would she be, married to me?" And he'd always reply, "That's why I'm asking."

When she was sick in the hospital, if I were discussing something with him about one of the groups I was involved in, he would say, "Drop it. I want to know how Mary is.

What's going on? What are they doing in the hospital for her? If you need my help, call me." You could always get him on the phone, and he was always there. When I was in St. Vincent's Hospital myself, he would either come in to see me or call me on the phone. When he came, he'd go from room to room—he never said no to somebody who asked to see him.

FOR HER FAMILY

Eileen White

For me, he was a boss, a friend, a colleague, a teacher, and a spiritual advisor. He knew the ups and downs of my professional life and my personal life. He buried my father. My father had Huntington's disease, and there was no place in New York to send him. We got to the point where we were taking care of him at home, and eventually we couldn't do it anymore. The Cardinal opened a unit of the Terence Cardinal Cooke Center, the old Flower Fifth Avenue Hospital, for people with Huntington's disease. It now has 50 beds. He did that for my family.

Wit

It was a few years ago, I think, when the National Endowment for the Arts funded a catalogue that described me, the Archbishop of New York, as a "fat cannibal in skirts." I only took exception to being called fat.
—*Cardinal O'Connor's Sunday homily,*
October 3, 1999

HE TOLD PEOPLE he had a "Phildelphia sense of humor," which in itself suggested he was making a joke that only he understood. Cardinal O'-Connor was a man of humor—irreverent humor, aimed at colleagues and at himself. Those who visited his residence or met him at a formal dinner often were rendered speechless by an unexpected aside or a flip remark. Yes, the Cardinal Archbishop, a man of the utmost reverence for God and his faith, had a comedian's sense of timing and an intellectual's appreciation for irony.

A FULL TABLE

On his desk in his law office in West Caldwell, N.J., Thomas Durkin Jr. keeps a replica of a potato. Next to it is a vintage black-and-white photograph taken in 1919 of his father and namesake, wearing the uniform of a Newark police officer. "My father gave me this," he says, pointing to the potato. "He also gave me the following admonition: 'Keep this on your desk, and any time you think you're a big shot, take a look at it so you don't forget where you came from.'"

Mr. Durkin's sister, Veronica Durkin, introduced him to Father John O'Connor more than 40 years ago. When O'Connor was appointed to the New York Archdiocese, Mr. Durkin's friendship with him deepened. He and his law firm, Durkin & Durkin, worked behind the scenes pro bono for the archdiocese. He had the Cardinal's private telephone number: "The Cardinal once said to me, 'Only seven people have this number. There's the Pope ...' I interrupted him and said, 'I don't want to hear the others. The Pope is enough.'"

After Louis Freeh had been nominated as FBI director [under President Bill Clinton], he and I were going to have lunch. After the arrangement had been made, the Cardinal called on some matter. It wasn't unusual for him to call, whether it was midnight or six in the morning. He suggested a meeting, but it overlapped with the lunch that Louis and I were going to have, and I mentioned that. Out of the blue, the Cardinal said, "Does this guy object to having lunch with the Cardinal?" I said, "Are you kidding? This guy would give his left hand, and maybe his right hand, to have lunch with you." He said we ought to do it. So I called Louis back, told him what the new arrangement was, and I thought he was going to jump through the damn phone. So it's arranged that the three of us are going to have lunch at the Cardinal's residence. Now, this is my right hand to the good Lord, over the next half an hour, I got calls back from Louis, and those now scheduled for lunch grew from just us three to Louis's wife, to Louis's mother, to Louis's father, to Louis's brother, to Louis's cousin who was a priest visiting from New Orleans to Louis's secretary to Louis's four kids.

In the middle of this, Louis said to me, "Don't you think you ought to check back with the Cardinal about this?" I said, "Look, I know him well enough to know when I have to check about something, and adding members of your family for lunch isn't something I have to check." So after this is over, I'm again talking to the Cardinal and I tell him about the new arrangments. And the Cardinal says, "Listen, tell that guy we don't have any more leaves for the table."

The day of the lunch, I had to be at the residence beforehand on another matter, so I was there when Louis arrived. He was with his driver, and he asks if there was a place where the driver could sit and wait. And I said, "Oh, the Cardinal has taken care of that already." He said, "Really?" And I said, "Yeah, there's an extra seat at the table because he knew you weren't finished with your invitations."

Wit ✦ *143*

I once got a call from somebody in law enforcement asking if I had ever met a certain person, who happened to be the chair of a major company. And I seemed to remember thinking that Cardinal O'Connor had introduced me to this person. So I called him, and said, "Some time ago, did you introduce me to so-and-so?" And he said, without batting an eye, "Yes, and like most other times I've introduced you to people, I've regretted it ever since."

In the mid-1990s, I served as counsel for a Vatican commission looking into a dispute in the diocese of Corpus Christi in Texas. The members of the commission were Cardinal O'Connor, Cardinal [Bernard] Law of Boston, and another bishop. We had to go to a meeting in Chicago, which coincided with the Democratic National Convention there in 1996, when Bill Clinton was nominated for re-election. During the meeting, we broke for lunch, and my friend who's driving us says he's made arrangements already for the two Cardinals and myself. He tells us he's taking us to a hotel dining room. As soon as Cardinal O'Connor hears that we're going to a hotel, he says, "No way. We're not going to lunch in a place where we might run into convention delegates. I don't want to get involved in that." This significance of that statement was that Bill Clinton was trying his damnedest to get the Cardinal to give the invocation at the opening of the convention. But Cardinal O'Connor had no time for Bill Clinton.

Anyway, my friend says he knows of another place for lunch. We get in the car and drive maybe four blocks, and we pull up in front of this Irish place, Captain Maguire's. I got out and looked around and thought, "This is the place we're taking the Cardinals to lunch?" The bartender spots Cardinal O'Connor coming in and I thought his Adam's apple was going to do a jig. Whoever expected a Cardinal to come into a place like this? And you know, it was one of the most enjoyable lunches we had. But if instead of Captain Maguire's, we had gone to the governor's mansion in Illinois or the White House, it wouldn't have made a difference to the Cardinal. He'd be the same person, and would act the same way, whether it was Captain Maguire's or the White House. That's the way he was.

CAN YOU TOP THIS?

Joe Zwilling

There was nothing you could bring up that he didn't know something about. Usually he could top you with a story. I thought I had him once. My third thild, Mary, was born at home. My wife went into labor and 40 minutes later the baby was born. We never got to the hospital. I delivered that baby. The next time I saw him, I thought, "Well, I've done something he's never done." So I tell him the story, and he says, "Did I ever tell you about the time I delivered a baby?" I said, "You're kidding me." He was a Navy chaplain in Maryland, and an officer's wife was in labor. He was with them in the car speeding to the hospital, and he wound up delivering the baby. Again he topped me. I did it on my living room floor; he does it on the backseat of a car.

THE JOYS OF CELIBACY

Sandi Merle

I met the baby the Cardinal delivered years ago, when he was in the Navy. He was in his quarters one night, the time when babies like to be born, and he got a phone call from a woman on the base whose husband was on a ship, who said, "I'm going into labor." In those days, of course, they drove wide-bodied cars, and he told his secretary, "Call the hospital and tell them to expect us, and get the car." As the Cardinal later explained it, they went under the first bridge [on the way to the hospital], and he heard "Ohh!" They went under another bridge, and he heard "Oh, momma!" And before they got to the hospital, he knew he would have to deliver that child. So he does, and now they're at the hospital, and the doctors and nurses come running about, and he tells them, "Slow down. It's all over." He had the baby in his arms.

There's a postscript to the story. It was a Sunday morning, and I was at the Cathedral, and Monsignor [Gregory] Mustaciuolo, one of the Cardinal's secretaries, came over to me and handed me two coloring books and two boxes of crayons. "In a minute," he said, "you'll see who to give this to." And then this lovely-looking couple with two children, one in arm and one in hand, comes walking to the first pew. After the Mass, as was customary, I was invited to the residence. As we walked in that day, I saw this same lovely couple saying goodbye, and when I heard the mother say to her children, "Say goodbye to the Father," not, "Say goodbye to His

Eminence," I knew they were special in some way. So then, when we sat down, he said to me, "Do you know who that was?" I said, "No, I haven't the slightest idea." So he told the story about delivering the baby, and explained that the mother was that child. And then he adds that after he delivered the child, he went to the nurse's station to clean up. He was then handed a paper to sign. He looked at it, and it said: Physician of record: John J. O'Connor. And he said, "I was just so happy that my name wasn't listed under 'father' that I just signed it." He then held his head and said of the two young children, "You know, they've been here for three days, and they're not used to these wooden floors. And you know, Sandi, there's a lot to be said for celibacy."

QUICK THINKING

Tom Durkin

In 1999, one of my clients offered to donate $50,000 to charity to commemorate my 50th wedding anniversary. I told them to make the check out to the Archdiocese of New York. I brought the check up to the Catholic Center on First Avenue. I went up to the top floor, where the Cardinal's offices were. He was in a dining room off the conference room, and there were a few priests in there with him. I explained that this client was making a donation on the occasion of my anniversary. I leaned over and handed him the check. He adjusted his glasses, looked at the check, looked up at me, and said, "Why didn't you tell them it was your 75th anniversary?"

A PART-TIME RABBI

Rabbi Klenicki

Once we invited him to talk at one of the Anti-Defamation League dinners. He was there to help present a booklet we had put out. During his speech, he told a story about how he once went to a Reform synagogue and he was the only one there with a yarmulke. Several Reform rabbis who were there looked at each other—I think they couldn't believe it—but everybody was laughing. The Cardinal had a serious point, too. Later that night, he said that he was in pain because there are Jews who do not want to exercise their Judaism because of assimilation or other reasons. It is their duty to practice their faith, he said, to prove that God exists and to refute the Holocaust. He sounded very much like a rabbi when he spoke. I think he just had a way with Jewish audiences. The crowd was all around him afterwards, shaking his hand and embracing him. I told him that if he ever needed a job I knew a congregation that could use him.

THE HIDDEN TALENTS OF CARDINALS

Monsignor Finn

He could be a remarkable rogue at times. He was unabashed with public personalities. He could tweak the beak of anybody without a second thought. It was never cruel, although I think it perplexed some people. And he appreciated humor in others.

Cardinal Agostino Casaroli, the Vatican Secretary of State at the time, came to New York for some official function, and the Cardinal had a dinner for him. Among those in attendance were the late Cardinal Manning of Los Angeles, the late Cardinal Krol of Phildelphia, Cardinal Law from Boston, and Cardinal Baum of Washington, D.C. There were also a number of auxiliary bishops and other priests, about 40. A pretty distinguished group. We were in the dining room on the first floor in the residence, and it was all very nice. After dinner, the Cardinal, in his devilish way, decided that he would call on certain people at the table to sing. He informed everyone in the room that members of the College of Cardinals had many hidden talents, as he would now demonstrate. So he started calling on the Cardinals to sing a few bars of their favorite songs. Cardinal Manning got up and sang that old Irish song, "Alive, Alive, Oh!" [The song is about "sweet Molly Malone," who "wheeled her wheelbarrow, through streets broad and narrow, singing cockles and mussels, alive, alive oh!"] Cardinal Krol got up and sang "Tiny Bubbles." The place was roaring. Then Cardinal Law sang "Simon, Son of John," a very poignant hymm. Nobody knew that any of these Cardinals could sing. And then Cardinal O'Connor, as he often said on these occasions, said that nobody could leave until they heard Bishop [Patrick] Ahearn sing "Danny Boy." Bishop Ahearn had a wonderful singing voice, and after he got through "Danny Boy" and one other song, there was tremendous applause. Cardinal O'Connor made some comment about Ahearn having a good voice although he was just a bishop. And Bishop Ahearn walks over to Cardinal Casaroli, stands next to him, and says, "Your Eminence, many a man has been made a Cardinal for far less than this." Cardinal O'Connor roared!

A SHTICK FIGHT

Ed Koch

Once there was a major fire on East 51st Street near the Cardinal's residence. When there was a major catastrophe, I went. It was part of my job. And as I arrived [he starts to chuckle], there's the Cardinal strolling down the block. The television cameras were already there, and the reporters, and one of them asked if the two of us could come together so he could interview both of us. And the reporter asks, "Your Eminence, why are you here?" And the Cardinal says, "I'm just a simple parish priest." [He chuckles again.] I thought to myself, "He's competition!" And then they asked me why I was there, and I said, "I'm here with my mobile phone so people can call their relatives to tell them they're safe." [Laughs]

The Cardinal asked me to travel with him to Ireland [in July, 1988] on a pilgrimage for peace and to pray at the shrine of Our Lady of Knock. And I said, "Sure." It was great fun to be in Ireland, and I tell people that I sat in that church in Knock for seven hours at a time, and after a while, those statues in the church began to move! I also had a rift with the Irish community during the trip. A television reporter asked me what I thought of the British presence in Northern Ireland. And I said, "Well, I think they're there as peacekeepers, trying to change things for the better." That got headlines back home. In the House of Commons, Maggie Thatcher commended me! That's all I needed. Members of the House got up and said I should be invited to Britain. Ay, gott! It was awful.

The Cardinal came home a day after me, and he gets off the plane and all the reporters are there. And—I heard him say this on television—he's asked, "What did you think of Mayor Koch's comment about the British?" And he said, "The dumbest thing I've heard in years." [Bursts out laughing.] At that time I wasn't so crazy about it. Now it's funny.

The other trip I took with him was when he was elevated to Cardinal. We had a wonderful dinner that night, and that's when he made the statement he repeated over the years, that only in New York could two people who are constantly suing each other be such good friends. That was rather sweet.

I would always go to St. Patrick's for Midnight Mass at Christmas. I don't think any of my illnesses kept me away. He would always introduce me, which is not so unusual, but after he introduced me, it would be followed by a comment. Something like, "There are 3,000 of us in St. Patrick's tonight, and many of you are not Catholic and will not know what to do at particular moments during the Mass. You may feel embarrassed. Do not. Look in the direction of Mayor Koch, and whatever he does, you do." And he had another one, which was, "Mayor Koch is in his seat. Let the Mass begin!" [Laughs] That was sweet. That was extraordinary.

BASIC BLACK

Patrick McKernan is the secretary general of Ireland's Department of Foreign Affairs. He is a former Irish ambassador to the United States.

The Cardinal was one of the guests of honor at a fundraising dinner for the American-Ireland fund in New York in the late 1980s or early 1990s. He was there in his ecclesiastical garb. Also at the dinner were Tony O'Reilly, the former CEO of Heinz, and his wife. As it happened, Mrs. O'Reilly and my wife were wearing the same exact black dress, even though they had been separately assured that the dresses they were buying were one of a kind. The two women at one point were standing on either side of the Cardinal, and Dr. O'Reilly said, "Your Eminence, they look like they could be your female acolytes." Here's this conservative priest, and you wondered what he would think. But the Cardinal clearly found this amusing.

KOCH VS. CUOMO

Ed Koch

When he did his first homily in St. Patrick's Cathedral after coming to New York from Scranton, I was sitting in the front row with Governor Cuomo and other dignitaries. I don't recall what he said, except that at one point early into the homily, he suddenly stopped and said, "How'm I doing?" Now, that's a phrase that has been associated with me since I ran for Congress in 1968, and even today people know the phrase. Everybody laughed, and then he said, "I'm not asking Mayor Koch. I'm asking the Mayor of Scranton." And there was a second round of laughs.

After the ceremony, I went on the receiving line to meet the Cardinal. Governor Cuomo, because of his rank, was immediately in front of me. As he gets up there to shake the Cardinal's hand, the Cardinal says, "Mayor Koch, it's a pleasure to meet you." I thought Cuomo would have a stroke. [Laughs] It's hard for me to believe the Cardinal did it intentionally. But then I introduced myself.

Mario Cuomo

Ed Koch and I lined up in the cathedral—and he always loved Ed Koch—after the Archbishop's first Mass. He was going to greet us. I had been warned by some people who said, "You know, he's been told unkind things about you. He's got to get to know you." So I assumed he would know my face, and the difference between my face and Ed Koch's face. But when he saw me, he said, "Oh, Mr. Mayor, it's a great pleasure to meet you." I said, "Monsignor, the pleasure is all mine." [Laughs] Koch couldn't have heard this or he would have made some comment, I'm sure. I got a look from the Cardinal. I never forgot that somewhat awkward introduction.

Wit

A CHESS PIECE

Rabbi Michael Miller

I told him once about something my son said to me about him. I had gone home to my wife and three kids and told them that I had just met with the Archbishop of New York. I was just starting to teach my son to play chess at the time, and of course his first question was, "Does he move on the diagonal?" The Cardinal had such a laugh at that.

Faith

God cannot be someone floating around in the air. God has to be one with us. That is the only thing that eventually responds to our needs, resolves our problems, fills out loneliness.

—Cardinal O'Connor's Sunday homily,
November 14, 1999

JOHN J. O'CONNOR LEARNED about the power and importance of faith in the row house he shared with his parents and siblings. His faith set him free, free to pursue and speak the truth, free to pursue his vocation without concern for material goods or temporal power. Whether in a Navy base in the Pacific or on the altar of St. Patrick's Cathedral, he shared his faith with all who crossed his path. And just as he placed his faith in God, he showed his faith in God's creation—human beings, who found, often to their surprise, that John O'Connor believed in them.

HIS RELATIONSHIP WITH GOD

Cardinal O'Connor appointed Sister Anne Connelly as co-vicar of religious for the New York Archdiocese in 1998. She acts as a liaison between the Cardinal's office in midtown Manhattan and the 3,900 nuns and brothers from 100 congregations who work in the archdiocese. She is yet another example of Cardinal O'Connor's willingness to promote women to positions of authority. "From my observations and from my experience, he worked closely with women," she said. "He took that quite seriously."

You couldn't be the Cardinal-Archbishop of New York if you weren't a person of great faith because you have to rely so much on God. You don't know what's going to happen—you have to be prepared spiritually, and you trust in God that whatever happens, you'll be able to handle it, no matter how difficult. And Cardinal O'Connor had to handle many difficult matters, all over the world. He was committed to his relationship with God, and I think he developed it over time, like everybody does.

I remember being at a special litugy when the Cardinal celebrated somebody's jubilee. It was a very spiritual experience, a holy experience. And when he held the Mass of Confirmation for children and young adults with special needs every Pentecost Sunday, he would be absolutely beautiful and real. He touched them and ministered them in a very real and compassionate way. You can't fake that. To me, that comes from a deep faith and love. We also had a Mass for adults with physical problems, and he was so loving. You can't do that without great faith, whatever your faith may be.

A FAVORITE QUOTE

Dolores Grier made history when Cardinal O'Connor named her as the first lay woman to hold the title of vice chancellor in an American archdiocese. She also became the first black lay person to hold such a title. Ms. Grier was raised a Baptist but attended a Catholic high school in Harlem. "I'd go to Mass on holy days with my friend, who was Italian, and when it came time to receive Communion, she'd say, 'You can't go to Communion. You're not Catholic.'" That changed in her senior year. Subsequently, two of her three brothers converted. "Then my mother saw Pope Paul VI when he came to New York in 1965. She was close enough to touch his vestments." She, too, converted soon afterward.

Ms. Grier holds honorary doctorates from Iona College, St. John's University, and Providence College, and is a member of the New York State Catholic Conference's Public Policy Committee.

The Cardinal called me into his office one day and he said to me, "What do you think is your best asset?" I said, "I like people, and people seem to like me. If they don't in the beginning, at least they get used to me." [Laughs]. He said, "Good." And then he went on to say, "You know, we'd like you to be the vice chancellor." I turned white, red, blue, green, and he looked at me, and he thought I was about to pass out. He asked me if I wanted some water, and I said, "Yes, please."

After a minute or two, I told him I didn't think I was ready for it, I didn't think I was the one for it. But you know, he pushed and pushed. One of the priests later said to me, "Dolores, remember he's a military man. He gets what he wants." I finally said, "Well, give me a day or so to think it over." He said, "OK, you can have until tomorrow." Then, I find out, he called an editor at *Catholic New York* and told him the story, but said, "Don't make any calls until tomorrow."

After I officially became vice chancellor, it was in newspapers all over the world because I was the first lay woman to be appointed vice chancellor in the nation. And, of course, I was the first black lay person, male or female, to be a vice chancellor. Some of the priests were happy because I'm not a women's ordination person. They were pleased that I wasn't going to be on their case. In fact, reporters would always be asking me, because of my position, what I think about women's ordination. The Cardinal loved my response: I said, "I don't think about women's ordination because we don't have it in my church." And he loved something else I used to tell people—you can attack me on my race, you can attack my on my gender, but when it comes to my Roman Catholic faith, don't even think about it. Oh, he loved that! He sometimes quoted that.

BUILD US A CHURCH

❖

Mario Paraydes heads the Northeast Hispanic Catholic Center, which is based in Manhattan. One of the narratives of 21st-century Catholicism will be the replacement of the Irish by Hispanics as the face of the Church in America. Cardinal O'Connor was well aware that the Church's future depended on outreach to immigrants from Central and South America—more Dominicans lived in his archdiocese than in any diocese in the Dominican Republic except for Santo Domingo. Early on in his tenure, he went to Puerto Rico for a three-week immersion course in Spanish, and he continued to reach out to this fast-growing flock.

One of our first trips together was to the Dominican Republic and Haiti. I noticed during this trip that this man slept almost nothing. He was an impatient fellow, who always had to be doing something, whether it was praying, writing, reading, talking. During this visit, he went to a number of barrios and met with all kinds of people who lived in shacks, in sub-human conditions. He asked, "What would you like me to do for you?" And they said, "We want a church." Nine months later, the church was built, in a little shanty town near Santo Domingo.

He returned to the Dominican Republic two more times, and during one of those visits he broke ground for a new children's hospital that he funded. He was very involved in Latin

Faith ❖ *159*

America in general, but in the case of the Dominican Republic, he knew that so many of the faithful in his Archdiocese came from that country. He felt it was part of his duties to be closer to that country, to the bishops and the people. He would speak about being known as the Dominican bishop, because he had the second-largest Dominican city.

The people liked him, because he was seen as committed to the poor. He was a rock—unbreakable. It was the little things he did that were impressive. He was always concerned about his relationship with the poor. He never ignored them, never abandoned them, never walked away from them. Quite to the contrary—he always wanted to be in their midst. He celebrated Mass with them in the barrios, and would hug them afterwards. Sometimes you could see tears in his eyes. He lived the pain of these people. From a human point of view, he was a remarkable fellow.

A JOURNEY OF FAITH

Dolores Grier

When my mother died, we waked her in All Saints Church on 129th Street [in Manhattan]. Cardinal O'Connor had just returned from his first trip to Russia, a 12-hour flight, and he came straight from the airport to All Saints Church to my mother's wake. I wasn't expecting him—he was in Russia as far as I knew. I guess they told him about my mother on his way home, and he came directly to the wake. You can imagine how shocked I was.

After my mother's death, the Cardinal could see that I was quite distressed. I didn't take it well at all. My mother was something else. She had gone to work in a city agency as a typist after my father died. When she was 70, they said she had to retire. She said, "Why? All my children are gone." But they told her she had no choice. So she did, and she went back to school, the College of New Rochelle, and got her Bachelor of Science degree at the age of 75. She was on the front page of the *Daily News*. I did a lot of traveling, to Turkey, to Brussels, to Germany—and all my traveling was with my mother until she died in 1988. So, anyway, the Cardinal saw how distressed I was after she died. So he invited me to join him on his pilgrimage to Our Lady of Knock shrine in Ireland. That was a spiritually rewarding journey for me. I will never forget Ireland. I truly loved it. I could have stayed there. At one point, the radio people were interviewing me after we got back from a short visit to the north of Ireland. They asked, "How do you like Ireland?" And I said, "I love Ireland, but I don't understand why my people in Northern Ireland are living like that." And they said, "Your people?" And I said, "Yes, these are my people. Catholics—we are all members of the mystical body of Christ." Oh, they were so upset, and the next morning the Cardinal mentioned what I said during a speech—he said something like, "Some of us said all the right things in Ireland."

Faith ▦ 161

ALWAYS A PRIEST

Monsignor Bergin

He was always a priest. Living there in the Cardinal's residence, I saw lots of people coming in to speak with him about some spiritual concern. World leaders would pass through that house, and so would the less-famous. He was forever baptizing babies of cops who worked the Cathedral beat. He would do marriage prep work and conversion work. He was never not a priest. I've been a priest for 40 years, but I never cease to be amazed at the pastoral work he did.

EMPTY SPACES

Ari Goldman

I once had a conversation with him about being a priest, and he talked in a frank way about how hard it was. He described the loneliness and the hardships, and at that point I put the notebook away and let him talk. He reminisced about being a young priest, how hard it is and how lonely it can be, and about the doubts that creep into those empty spaces when you're alone. Maybe in some way that explains his love for the public and for publicity, and how much he needed to be out there.

A PROPHETIC DECISION

Monsignor Kavanagh

As for his relationships with his fellow priests, in the beginning of his time in New York, I would say he gave
the impression that he was concerned with big issues, like social justice. He saw us as people who had joined the same
army, and our job was to work for justice.

But then, some time later, he made a prophetic decision.
He decided that one day a week, Wednesdays, he would make
no appointments. That day was reserved for any priests who
wanted to come in to speak with him. The relationship between him and his priests changed from being distant to being intimate. Every single priest in the archdiocese came out
of those meetings affirmed by the spiritual leader and brother
priest. It was phenomenal. Priests knew they could call him
and he would have the time for them. If some priest had a
family need, he'd be on the phone immediately.

He was especially kind to priests who were in trouble, or
those who were leaving active ministry. He made sure they
were OK, and he carried them on the archdiocese insurance
policy so they would have medical coverage.

BE GENTLE. BE PATIENT.

Mother Agnes

He had a great admiration for religious life. When I worked with him, I'd been meeting with him one on one, perhaps to get his advice on a sister who was struggling or something of that sort, and he would always remind me: "Mother, you must realize what they've given up. They have given up everything. It's so tremendous what they've done." It was a way of saying, "Be gentle. Be patient."

A SPIRITUAL GRILLING

Thomas Monaghan, co-founder of the Domino's Pizza chain, has devoted his life and his fortune to the propagation of the Catholic faith. As the head of the Michigan-based Ave Maria Foundation, a charitable organization, he has founded a Catholic law school in Michigan called the Ave Maria School of Law, has helped finance Catholic schools, and has started an organization of Catholic business leaders called Legatus. His work for the Church put him in touch with Cardinal O'Connor.

We had a reception in his residence for a group of men trying to form a Legatus chapter in New York. At one point, we posed for pictures, just the two of us, and he took off his little red hat and put it on me. I have the picture, and the hat, in my office.

After that meeting, he took me to another room, sat me down, and grilled me about my spiritual life, in depth: How often I went to confession and daily Mass, and about prayer and the Rosary. He seemed to be satisfied because he then proceeded to advise me about Legatus, and his message was that every great movement in the history of the Church has had almost insurmountable difficulties in the beginning, and then overcame them. I assured him that I was not going to be denied on this, that this organization would survive and thrive. Well, we did have our difficulties, so he was right.

He never asked me for money. He gave me an open invitation to have breakfast with him when I was in New York. But it seemed like every time I was there for breakfast, it was either on a Wednesday or a Friday, when all I eat is bread and water. He once said to me, "You never eat!"

He used to get on me about saying the Divine Office [a collection of prayers, psalms, and such that priests read every day for about 40 minutes]. He said that daily Mass, weekly confession, three Rosaries a day, and reading the Bible wasn't enough. Finally, after about three years, I started the Divine Office before Lent. I told him that at a Legatus function three or four months before he died—he was there against doctor's orders.

Years ago, I went to Lourdes with him, which was a nice experience. On the airplane, he told me that he spent 25 hours a week working on his Sunday homily. That's something. Another time, I flew to New York from Florida for a meeting

Faith ◼ 165

with him, and it was winter and for some reason I didn't have an overcoat. The weather was really nasty, and I was getting ready to go outside in just a business suit. So the Cardinal went into a closet and pulled out his own coat, and said, "Wear this and keep it." It's one of my treasured possessions.

BE FAITHFUL, ALWAYS

Rev. J. C. Williams

He once called a meeting of all African-American chaplains in Pensacola. I remember him telling us that we must be faithful to whatever faith we held. "That's what your calling is," he told us. That really inspired me, to be faithful to who I am and what I am. At the same time, he said, we had a moral responsibility to ensure that those of other faiths could practice their beliefs equally. He said we had three duties: to minister to those of our faith, to those of other faiths, and to those of no faith. This wasn't something that was merely talked about. It was carried out.

That, to me, was something. That spiritual lesson stood out: That we should be caring to all people. That philosophy shaped my own ministry. I come out of the Baptist faith, although I was baptized a Methodist.

When he was chief of chaplains, he saw himself as minister to the Joint Chiefs of Staff. That was unusual. He insisted that the Joint Chiefs find their own spirituality, and not only did he insist that they find it, but that they were in touch with it.

He made sure that chaplains were available to them so they could talk in confidence. That was part of his legacy, making chaplains available to the highest level of the military.

THE POWER OF PRAYER

Monsignor Finn

He depended on prayer. He was often off by himself in his chapel, praying. And he'd pray when he was on his way somewhere in the car. He didn't make a great show of it, but he did always find time to pray, whether individually or communally. Those who lived with him in the residence would join together in the chapel for prayer and Mass, but there were other times when he would be off by himself, praying.

He had been around the world, through his work with the military, and he had a lot of real-world experience with real people. He was wise to the world, and yet there was an abiding sense of spirituality about him, and a real dedication to his ministry. And it didn't have to be explained—it was just right there, and you couldn't help but see it.

HIS ROSARY BEADS

Eileen White

He was never without his Rosary beads. Sometimes, when we were in the car, we figured he was dozing. Then we'd hear something, and we'd realize he was saying his Rosary.

For our immediate staff, which was small, he was minister, priest, and spiritual guide . . . and tough boss. He worked hard and he encouraged people to work hard. And when you work hard for somebody who works hard, too, that's easy. What's hard is when somebody you're working for is sitting around doing nothing. But he worked harder than any of us. His schedule was a nightmare—his workday started at breakfast and went nonstop, and on weekends he was always visiting parishes. But he was so happy being a priest.

A SERIOUS, SINCERE PRIEST

Mario Cuomo

People didn't know that he said daily Mass. Now, I know a lot because one of his altar boys, a regular on Thursdays, is a very good friend of mine. He always said Mass in the morning. How many Cardinals say Mass in the morning? And he always gave a sermon! Now, I'm sure he enjoyed giving sermons, and he did them so well, but, gee willikers, what are you talking about—20 people, maybe a little more? Eighteen old women, five distracted people on their way to work, three people coming in out of the cold—and he's giving sermons. That's a terrific story. If you had written that story in the first year of his tenure, he'd have been a different Cardinal in the world's eyes. Instead, he was the quintessential, orthodox dogmatist for the Church. Which he wasn't. He *was* on the subject of abortion. Okay. And he *was* on the subject of gay rights, or the gay life and its legitimacy. But there was so much more to him.

I saw this on a personal level. My wife, Matilda's, father was murdered—he was bashed in the head, and lived for a while in a hospital, then he was gone. The Cardinal visited him and we didn't even know it. My mother was in the hospital dying, and the Cardinal visited her, and we didn't know it until later. He was a serious and sincere priest. He was also human, which I think is necessary if you're going to be a good priest. Because unless you understand my weakness as a human being, you're not going to be able to help me as a priest. To understand it, you have to share a little bit of it. So I think he was human enough to allow him to be a really great priest—he knew the temptations, he knew the suffering, he knew your insecurity because, like every other human being, he felt it.

GOD'S IMAGE IN EVERYONE

Joe Zwilling

He saw every human person as made in God's image and likeness. It was so much a part of him and his faith. That's something we're taught in school, and we say, "Yeah, everybody's made in God's image and likeness, thanks very much." But he lived it like nobody else I know, and it really made me come to understand what that means and how radical that idea is. If you really believe that—I'm not very good at practicing it, and I'm sure he would say the same thing about himself—but if you really try, then everything else falls into place as to how you need to live your life. That led me to try and put that idea into practice in my own life. It's not easy.

"PART OF MY STORY"

Ed Koch

The interesting thing for me is that whenever I speak about him, the tears well up in my eyes, and I don't know why. [Pauses, looks away.] I mean, I'm not a sentimental person. I am a feeling person, and I do cry on appropriate occasions when I feel overwhelmed by somebody else's grief or maybe my own. But I find it very strange that whenever I think about him, I start to tear up. I feel very sad about his death. He is part of my story whenever I'm asked to speak, which is about 25 times a year. I have a story about my stroke. I was taken to the hospital, and the first people who came to see me were my family. The next was Arthur Schneier, who is the rabbi of the synagogue I attend. He said, "Ed, I'm not going to stay very long because you need to sleep. But I want you to say a prayer that asks for God's intercession, in Hebrew and in English." And I said the prayer, "Heal me and I shall be healed, save me and I shall be saved." And he left. About 10 minutes later, the Cardinal comes in. And he says, "Ed, I'm not going to stay long because you need to sleep"—when I tell this story, I say to the crowd, "That's when I learned that that's what everybody says when they think you're dying"—and he said, "I want you know know that you're in my prayers, and if you would like, I will pray for you in Hebrew." And I said, "Your Eminence, I've already taken care of the Hebrew. Could you try a little Latin?"

A MAN OF PRAYER

Mary Ellen Keating

He was a man of prayer, and that spiritual side of him affected everybody. He spent hours of time alone in prayer. People in Scranton to this day talk about seeing him in the cathedral early in the morning, praying the Rosary. You couldn't help but be affected by his spirituality.

ALONE, AT 3 A.M.

Raymond C. Teatum

During nocturnal adoration on First Friday when the Blessed Sacrament is exposed on the altar, the Cathedral is open all night, and you'd see him there, all by himself. We, the ushers, took turns doing one hour each through the night on First Friday. I had the two to three in the morning shift, and invariably you'd turn around and there he was, sitting in the back of the Lady Chapel, all alone.

A COMMITTED PASTOR

Martin Begun

I was with Cardinal O'Connor when he dedicated a new surgical instrument at New York University Hospital. When I walked with him into procedure room to see him make the dedication, he solemnly declared that it was the first time he'd ever said a prayer over a machine. Everyone laughed at that. I said that we could put a person in it if that made him feel more comfortable. Without hesitating, he said, "That's a fine idea, as long as I can pick the person."

After the ceremony, he went to visit an assistant of mine who happened to be at the hospital. She was dying of cancer. He had asked how she was—he had met her at some functions—and I told him the truth, which was that she wasn't doing so well. So he went to her room, and knocked on the door. She had been sitting in a chair with her leg up. I said, "Edna, the Cardinal is here to say hello." The Cardinal went and got a hold of her hand, and asked how she was doing. He asked her how she was feeling, and whether they were treating her all right. She was somewhat speechless, and of course we were all very moved. She was so happy to see him, and was talking about what a great honor it was. He talked to her for some time longer, and told her to call him if she needed anything at all. It was all completely unplanned, but I think it was a great illustration of the fact that he was such a committed pastor.

Another thing about that whole exchange, the Cardinal knew full well that Edna wasn't Catholic—she was Jewish. Later, when I thought about this, his remarkable capacity to interrelate with so many people of different faiths, it just made the whole thing that much more important.

A MAN OF THE CHURCH

Sister Joan Curtin

There was a dispute over inclusive language, and he was being pushed by somebody who's no longer here. He was open-minded, but you could push him only so far. He would go as far as his vision and his beliefs about the Church would let him. But all the pressure wasn't going to make him change his mind.

Yet, I didn't find him closed. I found him faithful to what he believed he had to do, and what the Church taught. That was coupled with the fact that he was as pastoral as he could be when somebody came to see him. And to me, that's very much who John O'Connor was.

FAITH, TRUST AND BELIEF

Eileen White

The Cardinal had great faith in me as a person. He trusted me, but it was more than trust. He believed in me, he valued my intelligence, and believed that I could do the job. At that time in the 1980s, to have a woman as one of your most senior aides in your cabinet, so to speak, says an awful lot about the Cardinal as a person. It wasn't whether you were a man or a woman, white, black, or Hispanic, 25, as I was, or 40 [she gestures to herself]. It was who you were as a person.

PRICELESS INSTRUCTION

To the end, he was "Father O'Connor" to Veronica Durkin, a retired Navy lieutenant who served with the future Cardinal in the 1950s and became a lifelong friend of the O'Connor family. Veronica Durkin was godmother to the Cardinal's nephew John Ward, who died in 1997.

When I met Father O'Connor, I had recently been to a lecture by Fulton Sheen [the Catholic bishop who gained fame with a television show in New York in the 1950s]. Of course, everybody was so impressed with the piercing blue eyes Sheen had. I saw the same thing in Father O'Connor. I felt he could read my soul.

I went to Rome for the ceremony when he received his red hat as a Cardinal [in 1985]. He was wearing red socks, too, but I don't think he ever wore them again. That night, there was a reception in the Rome Hilton, and after dinner was served, they wheeled into the room a huge cake that was a replica of the Sistine Chapel, with white smoke rising out of it. The response was wild. Many of us thought that he might become the first American Pope.

One of the things he taught me, which is becoming timely at this point in my life, is that the acceptance of dependence with grace is one of the last lessons we have to learn. I hope this doesn't sound presumptuous, but I pray to him now. I think that's appropriate.

I benefitted greatly from his spiritual guidance when we were in the service together. Often on Saturdays, he gave me spiritual direction, which was priceless. If I were to sum up his counseling, it was to pray and to keep it simple. He told me that prayer had to be central to my life. And he spoke of the value of meditation, and the peace of meditation. I always felt like an F student, to tell you the truth. We prayed the Rosary together many times. When the two of us were driving, we'd say the Rosary together. I was always amazed that someone of his intelligence and spirituality would seek out a friend like me. I felt gratitude for his friendship, and it sustained me. In all the years that I knew him, and all the titles he was given—monsignor, admiral, bishop, archbishop and Cardinal—the one dearest to his heart was "Father."

He was a great listener. When he spoke to you, you could count on it to be gentle and unambiguous. He showed a lot of love, compassion, and mercy. In every sense, he was an imitation of Christ. He saw the person of Christ in every person he met. Everybody he met was a VIP.

Justice

There can be no love without justice.
—Cardinal O'Connor's ecclesiastical motto

CARDINAL O'CONNOR HUNGERED for justice, and saw in the struggles of labor unions, civil rights activists, and homeless advocates the words and actions of those Jesus praised in the Sermon on the Mount. The motto on his coat of arms reminded New Yorkers and the world that justice and charity were intertwined, that one cannot thrive without the other. He declined to cross picket lines, he sided with the unions representing Catholic school teachers and health-care workers, and he worked closely with those who sought justice at home and abroad.

"HE WAS ON OUR SIDE"

As president of an invigorated AFL-CIO, John Sweeney is one of the most important American labor union leaders of the last half-century. He and Cardinal O'Connor, the proud son of a union household, represented a long tradition of Catholic advocacy for the rights of working people. Cardinal O'Connor's pro-union positions were reminiscent of James Cardinal Gibbons of Baltimore, who helped persuade Pope Leo XIII to embrace the labor movement in 1891. John Sweeney is the philosophical descendant of Terence V. Powderly, the Irish-Catholic union organizer from Pennsylvania who transformed the Knights of Labor into America's first national industrial union in the 1880s. "My wife and I were privileged to be invited to his residence for Mass and a breakfast once, and I sat next to him at many dinners," Mr. Sweeney said, "He wasn't shy about giving you his opinions on any current issue." The labor leader shared many of those opinions.

We had two things in common: We were both interested in improving the lives of workers, and we were both Catholic. He certainly was encouraging, and he really identified with the labor movement. He often would reminisce about growing up in a union household, with a father who was a union member. He was very conscious of the social teachings of the Church, of its emphasis on respect for workers and the dignity of labor. It was related, in a sense, to his strong support for human rights, not just in this country, but around the world.

He understood the need for the aggressive role we're playing in terms of the global economy, our strong opposition to child labor, to forced labor, and how these issues are intertwined with trade policy. He refused to cross picket lines. The best example came when there was a strike at one of the television stations in New York. He refused to participate in a program because he would have had to cross a picket line to get to the studio. And he went to Washington to testify against legislation that would have made it easier to hire permanent replacement workers during strikes. He said that workers had a right to strike and exercise their collective bargaining rights.

As supportive as Cardinal O'Connor was, I know he had to perform a balancing act. He was close to many business leaders; when push came to shove, though, he was on our side.

DOING GOD'S WORK

Congressman Peter King

For him, the Republican Party was right on abortion and other pro-life issues, but on the other hand, he had concerns that people in the Republican Party were not supporting workers. That put me in an ideal position for him, because I'm pro-life and espouse the same positions on moral issues, and at the same time I'm a blue-collar supporter, a pro-labor union guy who stands with working people.

He had an almost fanatical support for organized labor. He felt unions were doing God's work even though he was concerned that some labor leaders were going down the line for the Democratic Party on all issues, even those that had nothing to do with labor.

There was always a basic decency about him. He was very straight, no-nonsense, and he had a way of making clear that he was the Archbishop. Even still, he didn't hide behind the mantle of office. He was what you like an Irish-Catholic leader to be—he would take a position and duke it out in the public square. He was the best of that generation of clergy.

"HE GAVE ME STRENGTH"

Dennis Rivera is president of Local 1199 of New York's hospital and health care workers union, which represents workers in the archdiocese's medical facilities. His members are mainly immigrants and members of minority groups.

I first met the Cardinal when I went with Jesse Jackson to see him in 1987 to ask him to intercede on behalf of home health care workers, who were making $4.50 an hour and had no pensions and no health benefits. Most of these 60,000 workers were women, the majority of them foreign born. The Cardinal did lend his voice on their behalf, and it led to a dramatic improvement—a 42 percent increase in salaries, and we created a benefit fund so they could have health care coverage for themselves and their families.

I really got to know the Cardinal in 1989, when I was elected president of 1199. He was the head of the archdiocesan hospitals, and they were our employers. We were having a contract negotiation, and I kept asking for more stuff. There came a point when the archdiocese's negotiators told me that the Cardinal wanted to see me at his residence. He said to me, "I want to tell you my philosophy, which is that I tell my negotiators to give as much as possible. I think we have reached that point. If you want to strike, that's up to you." I stood up and said, "Your Eminence, we have a contract." It provided for a 17 percent pay increase over two years. The Catholic hospitals set the pattern for negotiations with other hospitals. Those negotiations led to a wonderful friendship.

While he was ill, we had a meeting and he told me he was concerned that the unions were not sophisticated, that we had to make better use of the Internet and telecommunications so we could get our message out quicker. I remember to this day what he told me: "Young man, I will help you because I believe in you, but please do not become corrupt and do not violate the trust that the people have put in you." That meant so much to me.

He was a man of incredible moral authority. In my hours of turmoil, I would talk to him and he gave me strength and comfort. I became upset with people who didn't understand him and criticized him. Some of them were my friends. While the Cardinal and I might have a disagreement, I understood where he was coming from and I respected him.

When he was ill and deteriorating, the union took out a full-page ad in *The New York Times* thanking him for his work. His staff arranged for me to see him, and I gave him a framed copy of the ad. He was deeply moved.

In my house I have no pictures except for one—a picture of Cardinal O'Connor. I loved that man dearly.

HE PUT A FACE ON SUFFERING

Sandi Merle

He once said to me, "It's not hunger that keeps me awake, it's not homelessness that keeps me awake. It's the hungry. It's the homeless." He put a face on those labels. He said, "How can I sleep when I know that there are people sleeping on the steps of the Cathedral." They were never chased away. And he'd say, "I didn't choose to have a home on Madison Avenue. It was given to me. And I made sure that I took the smallest room as my bedroom. But how can I sleep?" And he'd look at us and say, "Do you sleep? And if so, how? Have you done what you're supposed to do today?" He was the only person in the city who had the respect of all religions, who could put together a prayer service in St. Patrick's Cathedral, and have imams, rabbis, priests, ministers—everyone represented. The last one he did was only a year before he became ill. It was nonpolitical, because, and this is one of his quotes, "Religion cares for people. And if you're going to say you're a member of a religion, then you must care for people."

A WELCOMING GESTURE

Brother Tyrone Davis

From the very beginning, he expressed to me a real concern that the black community feel a part of the Cathedral. He had a feeling, which was quite true, that some black Catholics felt alienated from the official Church, and felt very uncomfortable in the Cathedral. It didn't feel warm there. And he was very concerned about that. His directive to me was, "Let us do whatever it is we have to do to bring people together, to make them feel welcome." His concern, prior to the year when we had the liturgical dancer at the Black History Mass, was that there were more non-black folks at the Black History Mass than there were black folks. He didn't think that was the way it should be. His whole thing was, "If we need to get buses, let's get buses. If we need to reimburse pastors whose collections might suffer if their parishioners went to St. Patrick's that Sunday, let's talk to them about it. Do we need to have members of the black community as ushers? Let's do it."

As a result of these efforts, the Cathedral was packed with black folks on Black History Sunday in 1996. When he came out from the residence and looked out at the Cathedral, the look on his face was priceless. I came to appreciate the kind of relationship he had with leaders of the black community. When there was an issue or an area of concern, people wanted to meet with him, even people who others might have identified as very different in philosophy and approach. For example, the Rev. Al Sharpton. They all wanted to meet Cardinal

O'Connor. His motto, "There can be no love without justice," had a way of resonating with the black community.

THE FRONT OF THE BUS

The Rev. J. C. Williams

When Father O'Connor was named as the first Catholic senior chaplain at the Naval Academy, people in the Navy tried to talk him into taking a smaller house than the one he was entitled to. He told me that he listened as long as he could, then he wrote a letter saying: "I have no intention of riding in the back of the bus. Yours truly, John O'Connor." Then, when I became the first African-American chaplain at the Academy, he said to me, "J.C., I don't expect you to ride in the back of the bus."

"I AM A MORAL MAN"

Admiral James Watkins

In the early and mid-1980s, the National Conference of Catholic Bishops was preparing a number of papers, one of them on nuclear warfare. The first draft was pretty uninformed, and, frankly, was extremely tough in suggesting that anyone serving in a military that had nuclear weapons could no longer be considered a practicing Catholic. It was too much for me, being in the military. I didn't think that was the papal position. I wrote a very strong paper, which I delivered as a commencement address here in Washington, D.C. It was on the subject, "I Am A Moral Man." I went through the just war theory, on good versus evil, and made it pretty clear, without taking on the bishops, that we couldn't tolerate the loss of those who had read the first draft of this paper and who thought this was the bishops' final position. It was not. There was a second draft, and a third draft, and the third draft was published. It was acceptable.

John O'Connor and I collaborated on this. We worked together. I had called him in Scranton and told him that I was very disturbed by the wording. I didn't think it was appropriate, I thought we had a very defensive [military] strategy, we didn't like the weapons—we all agreed on that—but you're stuck in a situation where you have to face reality. The reality was that we had no intention of hurting anybody. Our idea was to preserve peace. We wanted to get rid of them, but a lot of water would have to pass over the dam before we could without placing the nation in jeopardy. We felt we came under the defense concept that had been cited by the Vatican in terms of what can be morally justified.

He worked with me on that. He had a lot of influence on the more conservative people on the National Conference of Bishops. He really was a very unique person in that he had a great deal of compassion for the poor and the sick, was a great defender of unions, and on the other hand he could be very conservative on other issues.

Justice ▧ 185

At one point, he talked about the book he had done, *A Chaplain Looks at Vietnam*, defending the Vietnam War, and he said he wished he hadn't done it. He was out there in the middle of it. He saw the trauma we were going through. We were out there, and we didn't like it. We didn't think we had a mission to win, we didn't know what the mission was—it was changing daily in the White House. At the time, it was tough, and I think he wrote that book with great feeling for the soldiers in the field, and yet, later on, looking at it philosophically, he thought he could have done better.

KEEPING TABS ON PEACE

Congressman Peter King

The Cardinal was kept up to date on the Irish peace process. He had a secret meeting with [Sinn Fein president] Gerry Adams in 1994, when Adams first was allowed in this country. The following year, he met with Martin McGuinness, Adams's right-hand man. I remember seeing McGuinness after the meeting. He was on cloud nine.

St. Patrick's Day in 1996 was grim. It was right after the IRA had broken its ceasefire. Adams was at Mass in the Cathedral on St. Patrick's Day, and afterwards, he had a private meeting with the Cardinal behind the altar. A few hours later, I marched up Fifth Avenue with Adams, and when we got to the Cathedral, we stepped out of the line of march to walk over and greet the Cardinal, who was watching from the top of the Cathedral steps like he always did. The Cardinal greeted Gerry and then me, and then I started to walk away. All of a sudden, I feel somebody grabbing me from behind. It's the Cardinal, and he's grabbing my arm. He yanks me back, and he nods to Gerry and says, "He's a good man. We have to take care of him." He said it with real sincerity and concern—he wasn't smiling. He realized the position Adams was in, trying to get the IRA back on a ceasefire and not get destroyed politically by the British. It was a balancing act, and Gerry was putting his career and even his life on the line, and the Cardinal understood that.

But it was the way that he grabbed me that made an impression on me. It was a combination of old-time Catholicism and his military training.

A MEETING WITH CASTRO

Mario Paraydes

He was very interested in Cuba, and his interest had an historical background. In the early part of the 1800s, in 1830 or so, New York had a vicar general of Cuban ancestry. His name was Felix Barela. He was a prominent Cuban priest who was sent into exile by the Spanish monarchy that used to rule Cuba because this priest advocated independence for Cuba. This priest was a philosopher, a thinker, a writer, and a great priest, and today he is highly revered even by those in power in Cuba—that is to say, Fidel Castro and company. Of course, they revere him as a patriot, and never mention that he was a Roman Catholic priest.

When Barela was sent into exile, he landed in New York, and he began to work among the Irish Catholics. This priest from Cuba became their spiritual leader. He established a number of churches and organizations to help the Irish protect themselves from the Protestant Know-Nothings. His cause for beatification was announced when the Pope visited Cuba in 1999.

The Cardinal knew that New York was connected to Cuba because of this man. He felt very close to Cuban history. We all knew that since the days of the revolution in Cuba, in 1959, the Church there was almost mute. There was almost no relationship between the Catholic Church in Cuba and the Catholic Church in the United States, much less New York. They were completely isolated.

All these elements explain Cardinal O'Connor's interests in Cuba. He wanted to help, to be useful and open a new path of understanding. So he went to Cuba in 1987.

As we were approaching the island, the captain of the plane received a message saying that the Cuban press agency was reporting that the Cardinal of New York and one of his aides—it mentioned my name—were members of the CIA. We landed in Havana, where the Minister for Religious Affairs—a member of the Communist Party—was waiting for us. I had met him on other occasions. I asked the Cardinal to remain on the plane while I went to see the minister and to ask him whether this statement was a message of non-welcome for the Cardinal. This fellow didn't know what to say, where to hide, and he apologized a hundred times. He said they would never insult the Cardinal, never mind say that he was a member of the CIA. So we went on to Havana and that very same evening we received a message that Fidel wanted to see the Cardinal.

The Cardinal had a celebration at the Cathedral in Havana already scheduled, and Fidel invited the Cardinal to meet him at his palace at 11 P.M. The Cardinal began the Mass at 9 P.M., and it was so packed, and everybody wanted to touch the Cardinal, and everybody was handing notes to the Cardinal as we walked through the church on the procession to the altar. I was walking behind the Cardinal, and I took one of the notes, opened it, and I saw that it was a message to him. So I began to collect them all. There were hundreds of messages. As Mass was celebrated, I read them. They had stories like, "I have a relative in the United States who is sick. Can you help me get in touch with him?" Or, "I need to leave the country. Can you help me?" Or, "We need medicine for so-and-so. Can you help us get medicine?" And it went on and on. Well, finally the Mass was over, the Cardinal was able to get through, and we rushed to the palace, and we got there by 11:30. So we made Fidel wait 30 minutes.

Fidel was very angry. He didn't show up until midnight, and when he arrived, he was very cold. He immediately said to the Cardinal, "Since the success of the revolution, things have changed in Cuba. And time is of the essence. It is respected." Ah! [Laughs] My goodness—that obviously put the Cardinal in less than a good mood. And Fidel went and on and on, for 15 minutes. He lectured the Cardinal about being on time, then he shifted to United States imperialism and capitalism, how the United States has caused all these terrible things in Cuba. He never stopped, and he spoke so rapidly that the Cardinal couldn't get a word in.

Finally, the Cardinal said, "Mr. President, you invited me here. I didn't ask for this meeting. I wonder if you really wish to talk to me, if you have anything to say to me. Otherwise, this meeting is over." Fidel began to lower the tone of his voice, and he began to engage in a real conversation with the Cardinal. It was priceless. From midnight until five in the morning, it was a pinball match. You saw two giants having a dynamic, intense conversation.

Part of the conversation was about the relations between the United States and Cuba. Fidel said he was open to establishing bilateral relationships. He said that everything could be negotiated with one exception—the honor of the country and the honor of himself. That was not negotiable. Then Fidel asked for the Catholic Church of New York to act as a third party to purchase medicines for Cuba. So, the Cardinal would purchase medicine, Fidel would pay the Cardinal, and the Cardinal would send the medicine to Cuba via a third country. The Cardinal did not know that that type of operation could violate the laws. We established a mechanism to study it. Later on, Fidel never really followed up, because he wanted us to break the embargo. That's what was behind all of this: to push us to break the embargo.

Then, he signaled that he wanted to send messages to President Reagan through the good offices of the Cardinal.

The Cardinal raised the question of the lack of entry of Roman Catholic priests and nuns to work in Cuba. The Cardinal negotiated the entry of 15 new priests and an equal number of nuns. Also, the Cardinal raised the question of priests going into the hospitals of the government, into jails, to counsel people, and priests and nuns working with AIDS patients. Fidel denied that there were AIDS patients in Cuba because Cuban people don't do those things.

At the very end of the meeting, the Cardinal raised the question of political prisoners in Cuba. Fidel tried to distance himself from the subject. The Cardinal persisted, and said he had a list of prisoners that he wanted to submit to him. Finally, Fidel accepted the list the Cardinal had. He went down the line, and said to him, "Out of all of these people, I will release, as of today, these 800. These other numbers here, this group will remain in jail. But all these others, you are free to take them with you."

So we set up a process in which the National Conference of Bishops of the United States and the Cuban bishops, and the Cardinal's office in New York, and myself—we began to take the political prisoners out of Cuba. Our commitment was that we would do this very quietly. No press and no manipulation of the information by the Cuban government or by our side. It was a very clear agreement, and no nonsense. Oh! This was incredibly successful. The bishops of Cuba were ecstatic with O'Connor. They had gained in one night what they hadn't seen in decades. Yet all this is unknown, except that the Holy Father and the key players in Rome knew. The Cardinal told Fidel he would say nothing about this.

Before we left, Fidel gave very beautiful gifts to the Cardinal—arts and crafts and beautiful boxes of the very best cigars. Fidel was simply touched by O'Connor, and from that day, he felt very comfortable with the Cardinal. And Fidel told me personally, "I like your boss. He is a conservative man, and I know where he stands, and I feel comfortable with him for that reason. And he's truthful."

"YOU'RE SAFE NOW"

Sal Tassone of Brooklyn worked in the mailroom at the Catholic Center on 1011 First Avenue in Manhattan, headquarters of the Archdiocese of New York.

I first met the Cardinal when he came downtown to visit Our Lady of Victory Church over near Wall Street. It must have been 1984, because I was working for RCA at the time. I went to the church for Mass during lunchtime, and stood up on the balcony. I got laid off at RCA a little while later and I got a job in the mailroom at the [archdiocesan] headquarters. That's when I met him the next time. I told him I got laid off at RCA, and I remember him saying, "Well, you're here now, you're safe now."

"WE DON'T WANT YOUR MONEY"

Monsignor Bergin

He killed us with his support for the unions. He was more with the unions than he was with us [the archdiocese's management]. His orders were simply to give the unions the best deal we could give them. We told him that we had to negotiate. And he agreed, but his philosophy was that we should give the unions as much as we could.

He was very uncomfortable with money people. If we had an event for wealthy patrons in the residence, he'd circulate for 15 minutes or so and would slip upstairs. I think the people knew he was uncomfortable around them. He would tell them, "We don't want your money, we want your soul." And those of us who set up the event would groan.

I remember listening as one of the nation's top executives at the time was telling him that he had to think about closing schools because he had to consider the bottom line. And, boy, the Cardinal gave him a lesson. He said, "We are more than a bottom line organization." He really gave him a lecture, dressing him down in front of his peers.

A QUESTION OF PRIORITIES

William Flynn

The Cardinal had big priorities, like education, which he put before the financial health of the archdiocese. He felt so long as the money was there, he was going to help the poor and the needy. I remember once talking to him about the problem of education, particularly in poor, urban areas. I said to him, "Your Eminence, with all of this work the Church does in these neighborhoods, had anybody ever said thank you?" The truth is, it was said in a manner that could be interpreted as meaning, "Why are we doing all this?" He stopped any further discussion with a look which said, "We're not in the business of getting thanks." I was reminded of what comes first.

SPEAKING THE TRUTH

Monsignor Charles Kavanagh

He had core values, and he articulated them well. And in the beginning of his time as Archbishop, he probably was a little too quick to speak out. He believed that if you tell the truth, then people will respond positively. What he didn't realize is that some people weren't interested in having a dialogue. He would wind up on the front pages of the newspapers, and we [the Church] can't win that battle. We're at the mercy of whoever is doing the reporting. Whether we're talking about education or health care, people often tried to make the Church look insensitive or autocratic. We're the largest provider for AIDS patients in the world, but when we enforce Church teaching on sexual ethics, we're compared to the right wing. It took a while for him to realize that not everybody wanted to have a high level of discourse. He thought people would treat him honorably, and when they didn't, he was hurt.

MASS FOR THE UNDOCUMENTED

Mario Paraydes

He was a strong advocate for amnesty for undocumented workers. During the last months of his life, he sent a letter to John Sweeney, the head of the AFL-CIO, praising him for advocating for an amnesty. He celebrated Mass for the undocumented and welcomed them to the Cathedral. He would tell them, "This is your home, you are here, this is your house, and I welcome you."

HIS GOOD WORKS

Mario Cuomo

Here's the most regrettable thing about our disagreement about what a governor should do with respect to abortion—it eclipsed all the other things the Cardinal was involved in. In 1983, my first budget had the first AIDS program in our history. He gave us St. Clare's as the city's first AIDS unit. He gave us the beds. He helped AIDS patients. Nobody knew that. And I marched on the picket line with him in 1990 during the *Daily News* strike. He was a great voice for the unions. He was a great anti-poverty priest. He was very much in touch with the bishops' letters, for example, advocating more government spending on housing and less on nuclear weapons. He was more Republican than they were, but what the heck, he was an admiral! I mean, when was the last time you saw a good, mushy-headed, progressive Democratic admiral?

He was Christ-ian as a Christian because he put the emphasis on good works. All right, once in a while he got ticked and threw people off the steps of the Cathedral [laughs at the exaggeration], but the frequency with which he did that was the same as the frequency in Christ's life when He did that. He did it once, just to show you he was human as well as God. The Cardinal had all these wonderful virtues. If you think about it now, he resisted the insistence of fiscal reality. He knew what trouble the Archdiocese's budget was in. A lot of people were saying, "Get out of the hospital business.

Move all of your money into schools, because you can teach Catholicism in the schools. You can't do it in the hospitals in quite the same way." He said, "No, I'm going to do them both." Well, that was his heart speaking.

Sure, you can fault the Cardinal for not being a better bookkeeper. But then there's the other side of the story. That you can love him for not being a better bookkeeper.

He was very old-fashioned—old-fashioned upbringing, old-fashioned Irish family, almost a Tip O'Neill type in the way he saw the law and society's obligations. The Cardinal was a lot like Tip O'Neill, I think, in his values. Now, he probably would have been embarrassed to hear that because that would have associated him with the Democratic Party, and I'm not sure that was his thing. But his values, like the bishops' values—if you put aside political questions—were very old-fashioned Democratic.

OUT OF HIS TIME

Nat Hentoff

Who remembers that the Cardinal was attacked by right-wing Republicans because he signed the bishops' pastoral letter on poverty which condemned the unequal distribution of wealth in America? He was out of his time in that sense. Remember, this is a guy who put up Dorothy Day for sainthood.

I was waiting for him once, and while I was sitting in an anteroom, I suddenly heard his voice from the outside. There was a hospital strike going on at the time, and the person in charge of the archdiocese hospitals wanted to bring in replacement workers. And I heard O'Connor roar, "Over my dead body will you bring in strike breakers!" That was the only time I ever heard him raise his voice.

The best description I have of him is that good old Yiddish word—mensch. He was a mensch. And he was an honest man. He would never spin the truth like most people do in public life, and he knew how to use humor. I found it interesting that when I was interviewing him for the biography and pressed him on women's ordination, he didn't run away from the issue. He said it could happen some day. He was more open-minded than people realize. He gave me a copy of the book he wrote justifying the Vietnam War in the 1960s—it could have been written by Robert McNamara. Then he said to me, "That was a lousy book. I got conned like everybody else." You don't expect to hear that from a Cardinal.

And in reality, he was a very good writer. It goes back to what George Orwell said, and I'll probably butcher the phrase: If you have clear thoughts, you have clear writing. Cardinal O'Connor had clear thoughts. I'd go to St. Patrick's to hear his homilies, and I was always impressed with his logic.

When the bishops got together to write their pastoral letter on war in the early 1980s, he was an opponent, at least in theory, to some of the ideas Cardinal Joseph Bernadin was pushing. [Cardinal Bernadin, who headed the committee that wrote the document, favored an end to the testing and deployment of nuclear weapons.] But when it was over and the letter was done, he decided the letter was right, and he pushed it.

When I was growing up in Boston, I got into journalism at 15 by working pro-bono for a woman named Frances Sweeney, a devout Catholic who ran a four-page sheet that exposed political corruption. She got angry because she saw that Boston was such an anti-Semitic city, and the clergy didn't care. She wrote against anti-Semitism, and the Cardinal at the time, Cardinal O'Connell, summoned her to his office and threatened her with excommunication if she persisted, which she did.

One day she gave us all a test. We were mostly all Jewish, and the test was something like you'd see in sensitivity training now. There were questions like, "What do you think of when you hear the word 'Catholic' or 'Jewish.'" Stuff like that. A few days later, she comes into the office, slams the tests down on on a table, and says, "You're the most bigoted bunch of people I know. Obviously, you're not anti-Semitic, but you have no idea what Catholicism is about."

I found some of Fran Sweeney in Cardinal O'Connor.

BRINGING PEOPLE TOGETHER

John Loud is a vice president of the New York Patrolmen's Benevolent Association, the police officers' union. A retired cop, he was the inspiration for one of the lead roles in the movie, Fort Apache, the Bronx. *He became a PBA officer as a member of a renegade anti-corruption ticket, ousting the long-time leadership in a bitterly fought election.*

After we won the election, we got an invite to meet the Cardinal. We went up there to his office, and he was really tired and really sick by this time. [Late summer, 1999] We didn't know it at first, but he must have been completely exhausted. But there was this radiance from him. I got the sense that this guy makes a really good friend and a bad enemy.

So I got to sit on a couch with the Cardinal. I was the old guy that had been there forever, so I guess I got the good seat. Everyone else was sitting around the room. We were trying to talk about how to reach different people, different communities, and the Cardinal came out with the idea that he wanted to be a bridge between the black and the blue communities—to improve relations between the cops and the black community in New York. He thought there was a chasm between the two groups and he wanted to be the one to extend an olive branch to both sides. He told us he thought that cops in New York were the best anywhere, but sometimes when we did something wrong we had to be able to admit to it. He said we had to cooperate, and if we were willing, that he would love to help.

Three days later, we got a card from the Cardinal, inviting us to come in and talk about things. So a month later, we had that meeting. We walked in and there was all of the PBA, and on the other side he had a whole coalition lined up, many black and Latino ministers and community leaders. I remember it impressed my wife very much—meeting him was one of the highlights of her life. As he walked toward us, from about 20 feet away, he said, "Hello, John." He remembered my name, and he made my wife feel at home.

We all mingled and he called everyone into a room. He talked to us about reaching out to people and trying to be healers. Everybody in that room loved the man, you could tell, and you could actually feel that this man could do good things. He went to bat for us, the men and women in blue, but his thing was also that sometimes you do make mistakes, and we have to build on the things that make us all better.

He actually did a good, positive thing there. Remember this was a time of extreme tension. That might have been exactly why he did this. He knew it was something we all had to deal with. He knew there was a long, hot summer coming up, and that one spark could have set off the city. But I think he just had his finger on the pulse of the community and that someone had to do this.

He was a guy who had the respect of the Jewish community, the Moslem community, blacks, Chinese, Hispanics. He was also tough, and I think you tried to put one over on him at your peril. Maybe he knew he was the only guy who could do it. He was the guy to try to bring all these groups back together.

HISTORY, CORRECTED

Patrick McKernan

Once, at a fundraiser, one of the speakers was talking about Ireland and America, making a comparison between the flags of the two nations. He said the flag of the United States, with its 50 stars, symbolized pluralism. By contrast, he said, the tricolor flag of the Republic of Ireland, with its orange and green separated by white, indicated a distance between the island's two traditions. The green represents Irish nationalism; the orange, loyalism to Great Britain. Later on, the Cardinal got up to speak, and he correctly pointed out that the Irish tricolor was designed to pay tribute to the two traditions, that it was a flag of peace and hope. This was an important point to make at the time, because the Irish flag had been banned in Northern Ireland for many years. In fact, he said, the flag is not divisive in intent, which underscored what some people had been saying for years. His statement reminded everybody that the problems in Ireland were not of a recent vintage. I was impressed by his knowledge of Irish history and his diplomatic skills. And, I have to say, he did me a turn by pointing out these things at a critical time for Northern Ireland.

Nearer His God

*But the souls of the just are in the hand of
God, and no torment shall touch them.*
*—from the Book of Wisdom, read during
Cardinal O'Connor's Mass of
Christian Burial, May 8, 2000*

HIS SUFFERING WAS PLAIN and painful during his
last months, but Cardinal O'Connor never
asked for a moment's pity. He joked about the
hair he lost and never regained after his radia-
tion treatments. He celebrated Mass, against
the wishes and advice of doctors and friends,
until death was upon him. The brain tumor
from which he suffered thickened his speech,
and the treatment he received disfigured his
body. He sometimes lost his place when he
read aloud or gave his famous homilies, but he
persisted. He explained why during his Sunday
Mass on Dec. 19, 1999: To his emotional con-

gregation, he said, simply: "I cannot not have Mass with you. I love you too much." He said his last public Mass in February, not long after his 80th birthday. And on May 8, in the splendor of the Cathedral from which he preached, his followers, his Church, and his nation stood and saluted his life, his good works, and his values. His friend Bernard Cardinal Law joyously observed: "I see he hasn't left the pulpit." For those whose lives he touched, John Cardinal O'Connor will never leave the pulpit.

NOT SUCH A BURDEN

⬚

Sister Joan Curtin

I saw a difference in him after he turned 75, after he tendered his resignation—which, of course, the Holy Father didn't accept. He seemed to relax and really enjoy it more. He had done wonderful work for the archdiocese, and you'd begin to see at meetings that maybe it wasn't such a burden anymore.

AN ABSENT GUEST

⬚

Howard Rubenstein

I celebrated my 45th wedding anniversary with a big party at Tavern on the Green [in September, 1999], and I told him about it maybe six months in advance. And he wrote back and said, "I'll absolutely be there." But he got very ill. I don't think people realized at the time how sick he was. Two days before, his office called and said he'd probably come. We even had the Police Department figure out where he would park. We did all the prep work so that when he showed up, he'd walk right in. Some of the newspapers reported that he was there, but he couldn't show. He was too sick. I was heartbroken. He would have been my guest of honor.

AN ACT OF COMPASSION

Mother Agnes Donovan

I remember the last thing he did for me. It was when he was ill. It was October, 1999, and my brother in Boston had impending surgery for a growth on his neck that looked malignant. I had said to the Cardinal's assistant, Eileen White, "Could you have somebody from the Church in Boston find out who would be a good doctor?" Six hours later, I received a call from His Eminence, who had taken the thing into his own hands—just what I didn't want him to do because he was sick. And he said, "Now, tell me about your brother James. What's going on?" And I told the whole story to him, and he said, "I'm going to call Cardinal Law [of Boston] and we'll find out who's the best doctor up there and we'll get back in touch." The next morning, he calls back—and it's clear that he, not somebody else, is going to stay in touch with me— and he said, "Your brother is to be by the phone at nine o'clock on Friday because Cardinal Law will be calling him." When I think of it now, I mean, this was a very busy man. Yet he would do this kind of a thing, and I'm not unique. He was very practical and concrete in his ways of loving you. It was rarely verbal. It was tangible. And the poignancy hits you later, when you realize what he did while he was ill himself.

A NIGHTLY PRAYER

Mary Dennehy

Eileen [her daughter, who was confirmed by Cardinal O'Connor at his annual Pentecost Mass for the handicapped] talked about him often. When he was sick, we prayed for him every night, and Eileen would point to his picture and say, "That's the Cardinal who confirmed me."

STICKY BUNS ON CALL

Sandi Merle

He had a sweet tooth, and he used to have a cache of chocolate in the refrigerator that very few people knew about. Late at night, he'd tiptoe down the stairs—he didn't use the elevator—to get a piece. And he loved warm sticky buns. I would go to Joseph Greenberg and Sons bakery on East 92nd Street every morning when he was sick to get those buns. Even though he used to watch his diet pretty carefully, he knew at that point in his illness, "What, am I not going to eat things with cholesterol or sugar?" So I made sure he had them there all the time. Sometimes, when he wasn't eating anything else, he would reach out and feel those sticky buns.

UNFINISHED WORK

Mary Ward

He always had a terrific work ethic. During his illness, he would be sitting in his chair at night, and he'd see a red folder on his desk. And he'd point to it and say, "See that? That's my work." He still had it on his mind.

A MATTER OF REGRET

Mario Cuomo

At the very end, it was really kind of touching. I don't think anybody knows this. I did an Op-Ed piece for *The New York Times*, and he read it and he sent me a note. I don't remember the exact words, although I should. I've filed it away with some other papers in a little drawer. When I drop dead, the kids will open it up and learn all these things about me they didn't know before, thank goodness. The Cardinal's note is there. What it said, in effect, was: "It will take me a while to find the right words to describe how I feel about this. Let me say for now, and only for now, that those of us in positions of responsibility are often misunderstood in the way we discharge our duties. And that is a matter of regret." Now, that's marvelously ambiguous, especially if you choose to make it so. And if you are desperate for consolation, for some feeling that,

"Hey, maybe he's talking about me," you can find it there. On the other hand, you can read it as him saying that he himself has often been misunderstood, and he regrets that. Or, you can read it as saying both. Depending on how I feel [begins to chuckle], I attach the appropriate significance to that line.

HIS WIT UNSUBDUED

Mary Ward

At one point, this was when he was very sick, one of his secretaries, Monsignor Greg Mustaciuolo, came into his room in the morning. He said, "Good morning, Your Eminence. How do you feel?" And there was a pause, and he turned to Monsignor Greg and said, "About what?" The two of us nearly collapsed from laughing. It was so characteristic of him, no matter what was going on, regardless of how sick he was, to find humor.

ONE LAST VISIT

Ed Koch

The last time I saw him was at a lunch he was holding in the residence for the seminarians who had graduated with him. It was the December before his death. I wanted to cheer him up with a Christmas gift, so I went to the Metropolitan Museum of Art and brought him a replica of the

Pieta. At his residence. I said to the housekeeper who answered the bell, "I just want to leave this for His Eminence." She said, "Come in." I said, "No, I don't want to interupt him." She said, "He has told me that if you ever come by, he wants to see you." I was still reluctant, so she went inside to ask him if he wanted to see me. She came out and said, "He wants you inside." So I delivered the gift and chatted with his friends. It was the last private moment I had with him.

It was painful for me to see him, because the treatment had so disfigured him. When I had had my stroke, I said to him, "Your Eminence, I would like you to officiate at my death," because I thought I was going to die. He said, "You're not going to die. But if I'm around . . ." [Laughs] I didn't officiate at his death, but I was there.

A FINAL BLESSING

William Flynn

Gerry Adams [president of Sinn Fein] and I visited the Cardinal when he was sick. It was profound. He met us in a little anteroom in the residence just off the living room, which was crowded with family and guests. It was his 80th birthday [January 15, 2000]. We were there for an hour and a half, and we talked about everything going on in Northern Ireland. He wanted to know if Archbishop Sean Brady [of Northern Ireland] was being helpful. The Cardinal's secretary and a few other priests were outside, and they literally had to drag the Cardinal out of the room. But before they did, we knelt down and got his blessing. And out we went, and we never saw him again.

ANOTHER FAMILY BAPTISM

Hugh Ward

I was the only one of the eight of us [the Ward children] who wasn't baptized by him. He was overseas when I was born. But my youngest daughter was the last person he baptized. We brought her to the residence in March of 2000. It was really heartrending. But life comes full circle. My daughter was the last baby he baptized.

A LITTLE JOKE

Joe Zwilling

The last time I actually spoke to Cardinal O'Connor was about four or five weeks before he died. I went up to the residence to see him. He was in rough shape. He was sitting up, wearing his black pants and a white shirt and a blue sweater. I don't know how well he could see by this point. Eileen White [his counsel] was there with him, and she said,

Nearer His God ◈ 211

very loudly, "Your Eminence, Joe Zwilling is here. He wants to see you." So I come in and say hello, and the Cardinal says, "Hello, Joseph, how are you?" Before I could answer, Eileen said, "Oh, you know Joe. He's got that high-powered job." Without missing a beat, and remember this is somebody who could barely raise his head, he said, "Well, I hope we're not paying him like he has a high-powered job." Just when you were about to pity him, he comes back with a joke, a little needle. I'll always cherish that.

That last memory of him, his sense of humor, is what helped me get through the press conference when I announced that he had passed away. What I thought was, "What would he want?" After that, it was easy.

I was in the room with him when he died, and I broke down privately, but not again until after the funeral was over. Even during the Mass, I was running back and forth. When they carried him to the crypt, I had to cue the sound man. I still had a job to do. But when it was all over, and everybody was walking off the altar and they were singing the closing hymn, that's when it hit me.

NO CAUSE FOR SORROW

Tom Durkin

I was at the residence the night he expired. I could not wish anyone to have a more peaceful and holy death. Cardinals Baum and Law recited the prayers for the dying for four hours. After he was gone, Cardinal Law grabbed me by the shoulders. He said, "The only thing you have a right to be sorry about is that we don't have him around to give us a hand. We don't have to be sorrowful for him."

A RIGHTEOUS PERSON

Rabbi Joseph Erenkranz

When I was called on to give a eulogy at St. Patrick's Cathedral [during the memorial service for the Cardinal given by New York's Jewish community], it was one of the high points of my life. I was asked to say a few words about somebody I had deep reverence for, somebody you just couldn't help but love. He was the kind of person I wanted to be. I would say Cardinal O'Connor was my mentor. We don't have saints in our religion, but I would call him a righteous person, and that's not a title you can give everybody.

ANSWERED PRAYERS

Mother Agnes

His funeral was quite something. From our experience as a community, we thought of him as ours. [Laughs] Or so we thought. It was just such a strange experience because

Nearer His God ❖ 213

all of a sudden the whole world had a part of this. And we were looking at one another and saying, without actually saying it, you know, "We thought he was ours. We didn't know that the whole world was going to take notice." All of a sudden the President and his wife were there, and they were never in the Cathedral when he was alive. And others of great rank were there, who also would not have been inclined to be there when he was alive. And we were praying from the bottom of our hearts, saying, "If this is so, let the truth as he would have told it, be told." We were praying and praying and praying. And when the applause was set off in St. Patrick's, that was the answer to our prayers. The truth was told, about life, about the preciousness of human life, without a word being said. He told that truth so well in his life, and told it one more time in death.

ALWAYS OUR PRIEST

Joanne Mohrmann

He was always our priest. That's a big, big thing to miss. Sometimes my sister Eileen [Christian] will call me and ask, "Just tell me what Uncle Jack would say to me in this situation." And she'll tell me something. But you know what he would say. I can always hear what he would say. I can hear exactly the words that he would use. Even when he was sick, he was giving me advice about my oldest son and college and girlfriends—right to the end, he did all that personal stuff for me.

A CARD PRESERVED

Hugh Ward

After my uncle died, my mother received his personal effects. As she went through them—this was really amazing—she found an Easter card the eight of us, the Ward children, sent him in 1963, when he was in the service. We all signed it and wrote little notes to him. When you think about how much he had moved around in all the years, and through it all, he held onto that card.

WHAT A GOOD MAN SHOULD BE

"Margarita"

We have pictures with the Cardinal, and sometimes I ask Patrick about the pictures, and he knows it's the Cardinal. He doesn't know what happened, but he will. The impact of the Cardinal on our lives, and not just when we needed help, was tremendous. I think his influence will guide my son's steps in his life, and in being a model for what a good man should be. I hope one day he will give something back to somebody who needs his help.

PEBBLES IN THE CRYPT

Ed Koch

I attended the Cathedral for a memorial on the first anniversary of his death. Cardinal Egan asked a dozen people to go with him down to the crypt. I did, and I was shocked. On a tiny ledge in front of the coffin area beneath his name were three pebbles. That means three Jews had been there to honor him and thank him. I told Cardinal Egan, "from now on I'm going to carry pebbles, because if I had had one, I'd have put one there."

Sandi Merle

When I go to the crypt, I leave a stone. Jews do that for two reasons, number one, that we are not forgotten. And number two, that's the way we build a monument, stone by stone by stone.

There was a reception in the Cardinal's memory sponsored by the American Jewish Historical Society and the Jewish Community Relations Council, and one of the speakers was Ed Koch. And he said that he was at the crypt on May 3 [2001, the first anniversary of the Cardinal's death] and he saw three little pebbles on the ledge, so he figured that three other Jews had been there before him. I didn't say a thing, and Mary Ward, the Cardinal's sister, started to cry, but she was smiling at the same time. We had visited Oskar Schindler's grave in Israel together, and we picked up some pebbles from the area around the grave, and I had put one there each time I visited the Cardinal. May I live long enough to fill up that ledge.

John Cardinal O'Connor

Rachel Fader was eight years old when she was diagnosed with a brain aneurysm. She soon began writing to Cardinal O'Connor, a friend of her aunt, Sandi Merle. Her first letter, in 1998, was handwritten; later letters were written on a computer. The following is a sample of their correspondence. (See also the interview with Rachel in the section "Inspiration.")

[Handwritten]

Dear Cardinal O'Conner [sic]:

I hope you are well. I am. I am taking an acting class. Also, I'm trying out for a part in *Fiddler on the Roof.* Aunt Sandi is going to write some music for my play. I want to meet you so much.

Love,
Rachel

[Handwritten and addressed to the Fader family]

Aug. 1, 1998

On this first day of August, as we head into the second half of a rapidly waning summer, I simply wanted you to know how often I think of you and how habitually I pray for you. I delight especially in the words in Genesis that the Lord remembered Rachel. Nor will He forget.

Faithfully,
John Cardinal O'Connor
(Sandi's friend!)

Sept. 29, 1998

Dear Rachel,

Do you realize how happy a letter from you makes me feel? Even though my good friend, your Aunt Sandi, keeps me informed about you because she loves you so much, there is nothing like hearing from you personally.

Fiddler on the Roof is one of my favorite musicals. Even if you don't play a part in this particular production, I'll bet one day you will be the star.

I hope you pray for me as I pray for you.

Faithfully,
John Cardinal O'Connor

January 19, 1999

Dear Rachel:

Thank you for being so patient with me. I should have answered your wonderful letter a long time ago, but I had to travel to Rome and elsewhere.

Your report card grades are terrific. I do not think I ever received grades like that in my own life.

I hope you're getting used to your new teacher. We all need experience, and hers will come with time, and with your help. Please give [her] my regards.

Say hello to your mother and father for me, as well. It is always wonderful to hear from you.

May the Good Lord bless you.

Faithfully,

John Cardinal O'Connor

Undated

Dear Cardinal O'Connor:

I hope you got my letter that I sent because I sent it a while ago. School's okay, but I'd rather be in bed sleeping or reading or even better, writing to you. I'm VERY sorry that I haven't written in SUCH a long time, but I have SO much school work. This month, our monthly project was to make a timeline of a famous woman. Then I have to stand up in front of the whole class and talk about my report. But the most exciting thing that we are working on in school is our slavery debate.

Our class is split into two (15 and 15), one side is for slavery, the other side's against slavery. I am against slavery. There are only about 6 people actually in the debate, while about 6 more are stage crew and the last three are actresses and actors. They pretend to be slaves in the debate. My teacher checked out like 10 books on slavery that has entries that real slaves wrote . . . We also have songs that we are singing. I am singing two songs, and I am pretending to be a slave. I think it's going to be a lot of fun! I can't wait! Nothing much else is going on around here, how about you? I just got my social studies test and scored a 98, so that was pretty good. But I'm pretty bored otherwise . . . I have you in my mind always, and I hope to see you soon.

With love and prayers always,
Rachel

February 18, 1999
Dear Rachel:
Many thanks for your letter and your Valentine's Day card. I am, thankfully, feeling much better. Your Aunt Sandi is very kind to let you know how I'm doing.

I'm sorry to hear that you have not been feeling well. I do hope and pray that you'll be feeling better and stronger soon.

I hope you pray for me, as I pray for you.
Faithfully,
John Cardinal O'Connor

P.S. (handwritten)—Your letters really brighten my day and my life!
October 1, 1999
Dear Rachel:
It was so wonderful to hear from you again. Please don't ever feel badly for not writing more frequently. I know how busy you are with school, soccer, etc. I am delighted to learn that school is going well.

I am feeling quite well. I am certain that your prayers and your concerns have helped very much.

Thanks, too, for proclaiming me the nicest man in the whole world. You are very, very kind.

Faithfully,

John Cardinal O'Connor

P.S.—(handwritten) I wish I were the nicest man in the whole world, but I thank you for your proclamation.

In August, 1998, shortly after Rachel began writing to Cardinal O'Connor, Rachel's mother, Ellen Cohen, wrote a letter of her own. In it, she told the Cardinal that she had been raised Catholic, but had converted to Judaism as a young adult. This is his reply:

Sept. 22, 1998

Dear Ellen,

Your gracious letter of 31 August 1998 reached me. Last week I gave an address at Clark University to mark the opening of a doctoral program there in Holocaust Studies. They tell me it is the only doctoral program in the world for that purpose.

The address was to a packed audience, approximately half Jewish and half Catholic. In the middle of my address, I pleaded with the Jews present to be good Jews, proud of their Jewishness, and with Catholics to be good Catholics, proud of their Catholicism. I urged both to avoid a "passion for respectability" in an effort to be purely American, whatever that is. Permit me to say to you that if you are a believing Jew, with the Jewish roots that you have, I urge you do be a good one. We best help each other by being truly what we are.

My warmest regards, and,

Faithfully,

John Cardinal O'Connor

Cardinal O'Connor and Ed Koch carried on a voluminous correspondence during their 16-year friendship. In this sampling, the Cardinal congratulates Mr. Koch on his victory in the 1985 primaries and offers encouragement to the Mayor during the corruption scandals of the late 1980s. Mr. Koch pleads with the Cardinal to make time for some recreation, and the two men debate the Balkans conflict in the late 1990s. The letters offer more insight into two giants of 20th-century New York.

September 12, 1985

Your Honor,

I once promised I would never run for mayor if you wouldn't run for archbishop. I have now determined that I will never run for mayor even if you do run for archbishop.

Congratulations!

Faithfully,

John Cardinal O'Connor

[Handwritten]

April 5, 1986
Your Honor,

You are prayed for far more than you realize. I don't call a man "friend" lightly. These are heartbreaking days for you. I'm here!

Faithfully,
John Cardinal O'Connor

On Dec. 29, 1989, Ed Koch wrote his final letter as mayor. It was addressed to Cardinal O'Connor

Your Eminence:

This is the last letter that I am dictating before I leave City Hall, and it is the most heartfelt.

Our friendship has been very important not only for me but also for those of my faith who were so pleased to see that the Cardinal and the Mayor of New York are such good friends. Occasionally we were in disagreement in philosophical matters, but we are both dedicated to all of the people of this glorious city. You honored me in a way I never expected. You gave me memories that I will treasure for the rest of my life when you said so many kind, loving, and generous things about me over the years. And, of course, the response of those who attended the Christmas Midnight Mass at St. Patrick's Cathedral will ring in my ears forever.

You said on a prior occasion that I don't have to be Mayor to have dinner with the Cardinal of New York. And so I hope that as soon as I have furnished my new apartment, you will honor me by coming to dinner with Father [James] McCarthy and the others who usually accompany you to Gracie Mansion.

All the best and again, many thanks.

Sincerely,

Ed

◎

The Cardinal sent flowers to Mr. Koch's new place of employment, the law firm of Robinson, Silverman, on January 4, 1990 and sent a letter to the former Mayor on January 5.

My friend,

A more memorable letter than yours I have not received in my years as Archbishop of New York. Thank you!

Through the media I am following your days of "transition," but my prayers and thoughts have been following you, and will continue to, in a far more personal way.

Our first dinner of the new year will come soon!

Faithfully,

John Cardinal O'Connor

◎

Their correspondence and intimacy continued after Mr. Koch left office, as this exchange shows:

July 6, 1992
Your Eminence:

Please permit me to take advantage of our long-time friendship to suggest a change in your regimen. If you are to renew your energy each week, you should take some time for recreation: the movies, the theater and the opera.

Let me make two immediate suggestions. Please permit me to secure for you, and perhaps Jim McCarthy or whomever else you choose, tickets for *Guys and Dolls*. That show is New York, and you would enjoy it . . .

I go to the movies every week, usually on Saturday night, but sometimes during the week as well. Why not come with me and help me review the film?

And, if you like the opera, let me call Nat Leventhal [the head of the Lincoln Center for the Performing Arts] and arrange to provide you with two seats for their next season. As you can see, these are all very catholic interests.

All the best,
Ed

July 10, 1992
Dear "Dr." Koch,

You are indeed a friend and while I am certain that innumerable clergy and hierarchy of the Catholic Church would find it amusing that the coaxing of a Jew was more effective than their own, still I suspect that only you could fully appreciate the almost full-time job that goes with certain positions that have "New York" attached to them.

I have decided, however, that if you reigned for twelve years as Mayor of New York, I will not do it any longer as the Archbishop of New York. Seriously, Ed, thanks! I really do want to take you up on your suggestions, although *Guys and Dolls* and the Opera would be more likely than most of the movies you have to see!

You're in my thoughts and prayers.

Gratefully,

John Cardinal O'Connor

The Cardinal never took up his friend's offer.

The Koch-O'Connor correspondence is filled with discussions of the day's events. In this sample, the former Mayor and the Cardinal exchange views on the Balkans crisis.

April 5, 1999

Your Eminence:

I read with great interest Michael Janofsky's article in to-day's *New York Times* which reported that "Last Wednesday, [you] and the seven other American Cardinals wrote to President Clinton and President Milosevic, asking them to halt military actions during Holy Week, a plea that was ignored."

You were quoted in the article as saying, "We cannot bring peace by driving hundreds of thousands of people into misery, refugees, many now starving, suffering horribly with no homes, with many members of their family ill with no place to go. We cannot find peace this way, not peace with justice. Nor can we find peace and justice simply through bombs. Life does not come from killing."

In the context of the article, it would appear that you are equating the genocidal attacks by Serbia against the ethnic Albanians in Kosovo with the NATO response which is without question waging war against Serbia. If you believe that NATO should not be engaging in a war to assist the ethnic Albanians in Kosovo, do you propose an immediate alternative and an immediate end of NATO's military actions? The Catholic Church advocates the doctrine of a just war. What essential elements are missing in the Kosovo situation that should deny NATO the right to defend its actions as those of a just war?

You may not have seen my recent column on the subject; hence, the enclosed. I am writing to all of those who were mentioned in the *New York Times* article, seeking their and your guidance.

All the best.

Sincerely,

Ed

April 19, 1999

Dear Ed,

Many thanks for your letter of April 5, 1999.

I have been preaching repeatedly (but briefly) and writing about the war from the outset, and have read your column of April 2, 1999.

If I were to single out only one violation of our traditional just war teaching, it would be in the use of what I personally believe, after 27 years in uniform, the grossly disproportionate means to achieve an end, however valid the end.

I join those who believe that Washington's and NATO's management of the war is frighteningly inadequate. No war, as far as I can discern, has ever been won solely by bombing. Demands that the refugees be returned to their homes, I see as completely unrealistic. How many homes are standing? How much of the country has been turned into wilderness? Have we simply opened the door to Milosevic and others to do precisely what they willed? I saw too much of the same in Vietnam.

You know well my passion about the Holocaust. If our intention is to end ethnic cleansing, we have adapted an extraordinarily strange approach.

Warmest regards, and

Faithfully,

John Cardinal O'Connor

In January, 2000, Ed Koch wrote a column in Newsday *entitled "Beloved Eminence Merits Homage," after a reception celebrating the Cardinal's 80th birthday. Mr. Koch included the Cardinal in a roster of "truly heroic figures" of the 20th century, including Franklin Roosevelt, Harry Truman, Martin Luther King, Nelson Mandela, Lech Walesa, and Yitzhak Rabin.*

The Cardinal acknowledged Mr. Koch's column with a letter dated February 2, 2000. At this point, the Cardinal's famously neat penmanship had faltered, and his signature faded into a scrawl.

February 2, 2000

Dear Ed,

It would be impossible to reflect adequately on the 16 years we have shared since March of 1984. Could any evening during those years have been more poignant, however, than the evening of your loss of a fourth term?

For me, it was an ever unforgettable moment to go to the Mansion, unannounced near midnight, with one or two associates, to sympathize. No. To show a "oneness" nothing else, I think, could have demonstrated. You were stunned, I think, perhaps temporarily embarrassed, but I have always believed it was at that moment a relationship began which has grown deeper and stronger as the years have gone on, for me a great gift.

God writes straight with crooked lines. After 12 years of extraordinary success, you seemed to have been sidetracked. I didn't believe that that could last for more than a moment.

Indeed, I was personally convinced that your twelve years as Mayor were only a preparation for what lay ahead. Virtually everything you have touched since has helped countless numbers of people, whom you might not have been able to touch had you remained in office. In "defeat" you won a great deal of freedom to do good.

I have said nothing of "Beloved Eminence" in major part because it is beyond description. Never have I seen anything remotely comparable. Never will I see anything such in the future. I will be having it appropriately printed, mounted and framed. It will become one of my most frequently exhibited treasures.

Please God, we will still have a long future together. I hope that I will see much more of you in the months ahead than in the months past. Let not time get away from us. We have too much to do together for the good of a lot of people.

Faithfully,
John Cardinal O'Connor.

ACKNOWLEDGMENTS

Every person interviewed for this book has my deepest thanks. Their stories of compassion, inspiration, and faith are unforgettable.

Some people who spoke with me deserve an extra acknowledgment for putting me in touch with others, or assisting me in tracking down old stories. Cardinal O'Connor's family—Mary Ward, Eileen Christian, Joanne Mohrmann, and Hugh Ward—generously shared their special insights. Nat Hentoff introduced me to Sandi Merle, and I now am in debt to both of them. Joe Zwilling of the New York Archdiocese, Eamonn McKee of the Irish Consulate in New York, and Kevin Fogarty of Congressman Peter King's office could not have been more helpful. Ed Koch not only sat for an interview, but allowed me to read his correspondence with the Cardinal. It was a delight to re-connect with two old friends, Monsignor Peter Finn and Monsignor Thomas Bergin, a couple of fine storytellers. Bishop James McCarthy, Monsignor Gerald Walsh, Eileen White, and Tom Durkin opened doors for me, as did Kathryn Murphy, Joe Conason, Maureen Connolly, Brian Mulhearn, Mitchell Moss, Chris Franz, and Dan Lynch. I am especially indebted to Steven, Patti Ann, and Conor McDonald, to Michael Zappalorti, and to Ellen Cohen and Rachel Fader, for sharing their poignant stories with me.

This is the fourth time I have had reason to thank Arthur Carter, publisher of the *New York Observer*, and Peter Kaplan, the *Observer's* editor, for their patience. They never fail to amaze me.

Tracy Behar, editorial director of Pocket Books, and Luke Dempsey, this book's editor, were enthusiastic supporters of the project, and I am very thankful for Luke's graceful editing. John Wright is my agent; more important, he is my good friend. Alan Joyce, who helped with the production of this book, had reason to complain, but never did. The same was true for copyeditor Jerry Kappes. Greg Sargent and Josh Benson offered invaluable help in researching this book. Meg Roland and Jerome Chicuara read this book in manuscript form and offered gracious advice.

My wife, Eileen Duggan, and my kids, Kate and Conor, make every day a joy.

Terry Golway
Maplewood, N.J.